E C **Travels**

Smara: The Forbidden City by Michel Vieuchange
Italian Hours by Henry James
Amyntas by André Gide
Pictures from Italy by Charles Dickens
The Journey's Echo by Freya Stark
Augustus Hare in Italy
The Spanish Temper by V. S. Pritchett
Italian Backgrounds by Edith Wharton
Along the Road by Aldous Huxley

Forthcoming:
Remote People by Evelyn Waugh

ALONG THE ROAD

NOTES AND ESSAYS OF A TOURIST

ALDOUS HUXLEY

THE ECCO PRESS

New York

First published in 1989 by The Ecco Press
26 West 17th Street, New York, NY 10011

Printed in the United States of America

Published by arrangement
with Harper & Row, Publishers, Inc.

Library of Congress Cataloging-in-Publication Data

Huxley, Aldous. 1894–1963.
    Along the road : notes & essays of a tourist
    by Aldous Huxley. — 1st ed.
        p.   cm. — ([Ecco travels])
    1. Voyages and travels.   I. Title.   II. Series.
PR6015.U9A8 1989   910.4—dc20   89-16865

ISBN 0-88001-230-7

CONTENTS

Part I: Travel in General

Part II: Places

Part III: Works of Art

Part IV: By the Way

Part I: Travel in General

ALONG THE ROAD

I: WHY NOT STAY AT HOME?

SOME people travel on business, some in search of health. But it is neither the sickly, nor the men of affairs who fill the Grand Hotels and the pockets of their proprietors. It is those who travel "for pleasure," as the phrase goes. What Epicurus, who never travelled except when he was banished, sought in his own garden, our tourists seek abroad. And do they find their happiness? Those who frequent the places where they resort must often find this question, with a tentative answer in the negative, fairly forced upon them. For tourists are, in the main, a very gloomy-looking tribe. I have seen much brighter faces at a funeral than in the Piazza of St. Mark's. Only when they can band together and pretend, for a brief, precarious hour, that they are at home, do the majority of tourists look really happy. One wonders why they come abroad.

The fact is that very few travellers really

like travelling. If they go to the trouble
and expense of travelling, it is not so much
from curiosity, for fun or because they like
to see things beautiful and strange, as out
of a kind of snobbery. People travel for
the same reason as they collect works of
art: because the best people do it. To have
been to certain spots on the earth's surface
is socially correct; and having been there,
one is superior to those who have not.
Moreover, travelling gives one something to
talk about when one gets home. The subjects of conversation are not so numerous
that one can neglect an opportunity for
adding to one's store.

To justify this snobbery, a series of myths
has gradually been elaborated. The places
which it is socially smart to have visited are
aureoled with glamour, till they are made to
appear, for those who have not been there,
like so many fabled Babylons or Bagdads.
Those who have travelled have a personal
interest in cultivating and disseminating
these fables. For if Paris and Monte Carlo
are really so marvellous as it is generally
supposed, by the inhabitants of Bradford
or Milwaukee, of Tomsk and Bergen, that
they are,—why, then, the merit of the
travellers who have actually visited these
places is the greater and their superiority

over the stay-at-homes the more enormous. It is for this reason (and because they pay the hotel proprietors and the steamship companies) that the fables are studiously kept alive.

Few things are more pathetic than the spectacle of inexperienced travellers, brought up on these myths, desperately doing their best to make external reality square with fable. It is for the sake of the myths and, less consciously, in the name of snobbery that they left their homes; to admit disappointment in the reality would be to admit their own foolishness in having believed the fables and would detract from their merit in having undertaken the pilgrimage. Out of the hundreds of thousands of Anglo-Saxons who frequent the night-clubs and dancing-saloons of Paris, there are a good many, no doubt, who genuinely like that sort of thing. But there are also very many who do not. In their hearts, secretly, they are bored and a little disgusted. But they have been brought up to believe in a fabulous "Gay Paree," where everything is deliriously exciting and where alone it is possible to see what is technically known as Life. Conscientiously, therefore, they strive, when they come to Paris, to be gay. Night after night the dance halls and the bordellos are thronged by serious young

compatriots of Emerson and Matthew
Arnold, earnestly engaged in trying to see
life, neither very steadily nor whole, through
the ever-thickening mists of Heidsieck and
Roederer.

Still more courageously determined are
their female companions; for they, mostly
(unless they are extremely "modern"), have
not the Roederer to assist them in finding
Paris gay. The saddest sight I ever saw was
in a Montmartre *boîte* at about five o'clock
of an autumn morning. At a table in a
corner of the hall sat three young American
girls, quite unattended, adventurously seeing life by themselves. In front of them, on
the table, stood the regulation bottles of
champagne; but for preference—perhaps on
principle—they were sipping lemonade. The
jazz band played on monotonously; the tired
drummer nodded over his drums, the saxo-
phonist yawned into his saxophone. In
couples, in staggering groups, the guests departed. But grimly, indomitably, in spite of
their fatigue, in spite of the boredom which
so clearly expressed itself on their charming
and ingenuous faces, the three young girls
sat on. They were still there when I left
at sunrise. What stories, I reflected, they
would tell when they got home again! And
how envious they would make their un-

travelled friends. "Paris is just wonderful. . . ."

To the Parisians, the fable brings in several hundred milliards of good money.
They give it a generous publicity; business
is business. But if I were the manager of a
Montmartre dancing-saloon, I think I should
tell my waiters to act their gay parts with a
little more conviction. "My men," I should
say to them, "you ought to look as though
you believed in the fable out of which we
make our living. Smile, be merry. Your
present expression, which is a mingling of
weariness, disgusted contempt for your
clients and cynical rapacity is not inspiring.
One day the clients might be sober enough
to notice it. And where should we be
then?"

But Paris and Monte Carlo are not the
only resorts of pilgrimage. There are also
Rome and Florence. There are picture galleries, churches and ruins as well as shops
and casinos. And the snobbery which de-
crees that one must like Art—or, to be more
accurate, that one should have visited the
places where Art is to be seen—is almost as
tyrannous as that which bids one visit the
places where one can see Life.

All of us are more or less interested in
Life—even in that rather smelly slice of it

that is to be found in Montmartre. But a taste for Art—or at any rate the sort of art that is found in galleries and churches—is by no means universal. Hence the case of the poor tourists who, from motives of snobbery, visit Rome and Florence, is even more pathetic than the case of those who repair for the same reasons to Paris and Monte Carlo. Tourists "doing" a church wear a mask of dutiful interest; but what lassitude, what utter weariness of spirit looks out, too often, at their eyes! And the weariness is felt, within, still more acutely because, precisely, of the necessity of simulating this rapt attentiveness, of even going hypocritically into raptures over the things that are starred in the Baedeker. There come moments when flesh and blood can stand the strain no longer. Philistinism absolutely refuses to pay the tribute it owes to taste. Exasperated and defiant, the tourist swears that he won't so much as put his nose inside another church, preferring to spend his days in the lounge of the hotel, reading the continental *Daily Mail*.

I remember witnessing one of these rebellions at Venice. A motor boat company was advertising afternoon excursions to the island of Torcello. We booked our seats and at the appointed time set off, in com-

pany with seven or eight other tourists.
Romantic in its desolation, Torcello rose out
of the lagoon. The boatmen drew up at the
side of a mouldering jetty. A quarter of a
mile away, through the fields, stood the
church. It contains some of the most beautiful mosaics in Italy. We climbed on shore
—all of us with the exception of one strong-
minded American couple who, on learning
that the object of interest on this island was
only another church, decided to remain comfortably seated in the boat till the rest of
the party should return. I admired them for
their firmness and their honesty. But at the
same time, it seemed to me rather a melancholy thing that they should have come all
this way and spent all that money, merely
for the pleasure of sitting in a motor boat
tied to a rotting wharf. And then they were
only at Venice. Their Italian ordeal had
hardly begun. Padua, Ferrara, Ravenna,
Bologna, Florence, Siena, Perugia, Assisi and
Rome, with all their innumerable churches
and pictures, had still to be looked at, before—the blessed goal of Naples finally
reached—they could be permitted to take the
liner home again across the Atlantic. Poor
slaves, I thought; and of how exacting a
master!

We call such people travellers because

they do not stay at home. But they are not genuine travellers, not travellers born. For they travel, not for travelling's sake, but for convention's. They set out, nourished on fables and fantastical hopes, to return, whether they avow it or not, disappointed. Their interest in the real and actual being insufficiently lively, they hanker after mythology, and the facts, however curious, beautiful and varied, are a disillusionment. It is only the society of their fellow-tourists, with whom they conspire, every now and then, to make a little oasis of home in the foreign wilderness, coupled with the consciousness of a social duty done, that keeps them even moderately cheerful in the face of the depressing facts of travel.

Your genuine traveller, on the other hand, is so much interested in real things that he does not find it necessary to believe in fables. He is insatiably curious, he loves what is unfamiliar for the sake of its unfamiliarity, he takes pleasure in every manifestation of beauty. It would be absurd, of course, to say that he is never bored. For it is practically impossible to travel without being sometimes bored. For the tourist, a large part of almost every day is necessarily empty. Much time, to begin with, must be spent in merely getting from place to place.

And when the sights have been seen, the sight-seer finds himself physically weary and with nothing particular to do. At home, among one's regular occupations, one is never bored. Ennui is essentially a holiday feeling. (Is it not the chronic disease of the leisured?) It is for that very reason that your true traveller finds boredom rather agreeable than painful. It is the symbol of his liberty—his excessive freedom. He accepts his boredom, when it comes, not merely philosophically, but almost with pleasure.

For the born traveller, travelling is a besetting vice. Like other vices it is imperious, demanding its victim's time, money, energy and the sacrifice of his comfort. It claims; and the born traveller gives, willingly, even eagerly. Most vices, it may be added parenthetically, demand considerable self-sacrifices. There is no greater mistake than to suppose that a vicious life is a life of uninterrupted pleasure. It is a life almost as wearisome and painful—if strenuously led—as Christian's in *The Pilgrim's Progress*. The chief difference between Christian and the vicious man is that the first gets something out of his hardships—gets it here and now in the shape of a certain spiritual well-being, to say nothing of what he may get in that sadly problematical Jerusalem beyond the river—while the second gets nothing, except, perhaps, gout and general paralysis of the insane.

The vice of travelling, it is true, does not necessarily bring with it these two particular diseases; nor indeed any diseases at all, unless your wanderings take you as far as the tropics. No bodily diseases; for travelling is not a vice of the body (which it mortifies) but of the mind. Your traveller-for-travelling's-sake is like your desultory reader—a man addicted to mental self-indulgence.

Like all other vicious men, the reader and the traveller have a whole armoury of justifications with which to defend themselves. Reading and travelling, they say, broaden the mind, stimulate imagination, are a liberal education. And so on. These are specious arguments; but nobody is very much impressed by them. For though it may be quite true that, for certain people, desultory reading and aimless travelling are richly educative, it is not for that reason that most true readers and travellers born indulge their tastes. We read and travel, not that we may broaden and enrich our minds, but that we may pleasantly forget they exist. We love reading and travelling because they are the most delightful of all the many substitutes for thought. Sophisticated and some-

what rarefied substitutes. That is why they
are not every man's diversion. The congenital reader or traveller is one of those
more fastidious spirits who cannot find the
distractions they require in betting, mah-
jong, drink, golf or fox-trots.

There exist a few, a very few, who travel
and, for that matter, who read, with purpose
and a definite system. This is a morally
admirable class. And it is the class to which,
in general, the people who achieve something
in the world belong. Not always, however,
by any means. For, alas, one may have a
high purpose and a fine character, but no
talent. Some of the most self-indulgent and
aimless of travellers and readers have known
how to profit by their vices. Desultory reading was Dr. Johnson's besetting sin; he read
every book that came under his hand and
none to the end. And yet his achievement
was not small. And there are frivolous
travellers, like Beckford, who have gone
about the world, indulging their wanton
curiosity, to almost as good purpose. Virtue
is its own reward; but the grapes which
talent knows how to pluck—are they not a
little sour?

With me, travelling is frankly a vice.
The temptation to indulge in it is one which
I find almost as hard to resist as the temp-

tation to read promiscuously, omnivorously and without purpose. From time to time, it is true, I make a desperate resolution to mend my ways. I sketch out programmes of useful, serious reading; I try to turn my rambling voyages into systematic tours through the history of art and civilization. But without much success. After a little I relapse into my old bad ways. Deplorable weakness! I try to comfort myself with the hope that even my vices may be of some profit to me.

WANDER-BIRDS

FAIR-HAIRED, bare-headed, with faces burned darker than their hair, they trudge along the dusty roads. They wear shorts; their Tyrolean knees are brown. Enormous boots, heavy with nails, click metallically over the flagstones of the churches into which, conscientious *Kunstforschers*, they penetrate. On their backs they carry knapsacks and in their hands, sometimes a stick, sometimes a stout umbrella; I have seen them making the ascent of the Viale dei Colli at Florence with ice-axes. They are the Wander-Birds, and they come, as their name (so romantic and applied so unironically), their Schillerian name too manifestly proclaims, from Germany. Many of them have walked all the way, across the Alps from Berlin to Taranto and back, with no money, living on bread and water, sleeping in barns or by the road-side. Adventurous and hardy youths! I feel the profoundest admiration for them. I even envy them, wishing that I possessed their energy, their hardiness. But I do not imitate them.

21

"The saints of old," says the hymnologist,
    "went up to Heaven
With sorrow, toil and pain.
Lord, unto us may strength be given
To follow in the train."

For me, I confess, even the train has become
a means of travelling too inconvenient to
be much employed. I would amend the last
two lines of the hymn to, "Lord, unto us
may wealth be given to follow in the car."
The prayer has been granted—partially, at
any rate; for whether a ten horse power
Citroen can really be called a car is ques-
tionable. Owners of Napiers, Vauxhalls,
Delages or Voisins, would certainly deny
it. I shall not argue the point. All I claim
for the ten horse power Citroen is this: that
it works. In a modest and unassuming way,
not very rapidly, indeed, but steadily and
reliably, it takes one about. This particular
specimen has carried us a good many thousand miles over the roads of Italy, France,
Belgium and Holland; which, for all who
are acquainted with those roads, is saying
a good deal.

At this point, if I had any strength of
mind, I should stop talking about Citroens
and return to higher themes. But the temptation of talking about cars, when one has a
car, is quite irresistible. Before I bought

a Citroen no subject had less interest for me; none, now, has more. I can talk for hours about motors with other car owners. And I am ruthlessly prepared to bore the non-motorist by talking interminably of this delightful subject even to him. I waste much precious time reading the motoring papers, study passionately the news from the racing tracks, gravely peruse technical lucubrations which I do not understand. It is a madness, but a delightful one.

The spiritual effects of being a car-owner are not, I notice, entirely beneficial. Introspection and the conversation of other motorists have shown me, indeed, that car-owning may have the worst effect on the character. To begin with every car-owner is a liar. He cannot tell the truth about his machine. He exaggerates his speed, the number of miles he goes to the gallon of petrol, his prowess as a hill climber. In the heat of conversation I myself have erred in this respect, more than once; and even coolly, with malice aforethought, I have given utterance, on this subject, to frigid and calculated lies. They do not weigh very heavily on my conscience. I am no casuist, but it seems to me that a lie which one tells, expecting nobody to believe it, is venial. The motorist, like the fisherman, never really supposes that his vaunts will be believed. Myself, I have long ceased to give the slightest credit to anything my fellow-motorists may tell me. My last vestige of confidence was destroyed by the Belgian driver who told me that two hours were ample time to allow for the journey from Brussels to Ostend; he himself, he declared, did it constantly and never took more. I trusted him and did not consult the road book. If I had, I should have found that the distance from Brussels to Ostend is something over seventy miles, that the road is cobbled all the way and badly cobbled at that, and that one has to pass through three large towns and about twenty villages. As it was we started late in the afternoon and were hopelessly benighted. Now, when motorists tell me how long it takes them to get from one place to another, I add on, according to their character, from thirty to sixty per cent. to the figure they mention. In this way I reach approximate truth.

Another horrible sin encouraged by the owning of an automobile, particularly of a small automobile, is envy. What bitter discontentment fills the mind of the 10 H.P. man as the 40 H.P. shoots silently past him! How fiercely he loathes the owner of the larger machine! What envy and covetousness possess him! In a flat country one envies less than in a hilly. For on the flat even the little car can do quite creditably enough to keep up its owner's self-esteem. It is in a mountainous country, like Italy, where the roads are constantly running up to two or three thousand feet and down again, that the deadly sin of envy really flourishes. For there the little car must abjectly acknowledge its littleness. The superiority of 40 H.P. over 10 H.P. is only too painfully apparent. It was on the Mont Cenis that the cup of our humiliation flowed over and the blackest envy filled our souls. We had started from Turin. For the first thirty miles the road is perfectly flat. We rolled along it in very dashing style; the smaller Fiats ate our dust. In front of us, like an immense uneven wall, the Alps rose suddenly out of the plain. Susa lies at the head of a long flat-bottomed valley that leads into the heart of the hills. You pass through the town and then, suddenly, without warning, the road begins to climb, steeply. It goes on climbing without respite for the next fifteen miles. The top of the pass is six thousand five hundred feet above the sea. The Citroen went into second and remained there; slowly we puffed up the long ascent. We had gone about a mile, when we became aware of a noise coming up from the valley, a noise like the noise of massed machine-guns. It grew louder and louder. A minute later a huge red Alfa Romeo road racer, looking suspiciously like the machine that had just won the Grand Prix d' Europe, roared past at a speed that cannot have been less than fifty miles an hour. It was evidently being driven by a genius; for, looking up, we saw the scarlet monster negotiating turn after hairpin turn in the zigzag road above us without once abating its speed by one mile an hour. In another thirty seconds it was out of sight. The noise of it solemnly reverberated among the mountains, like thunder. Slowly we puffed on. Half an hour later we met the red terror descending; round the corners it showed the same disregard for the elementary laws of dynamics as it had shown on the way up. We imagined that we had seen the last of it. But waiting at the Italian custom house while the officer in charge examined our papers—a process which, as at all custom houses, took a very long time—we heard, far off, a familiar sound. In a few minutes the sound became deafening. Like a huge red rocket, trailing behind it a cloud of smoke, the Alfa Romeo passed at the head of its white dust. "They're doing hill-climbing tests," the soldier on guard explained.

We set out once more. The custom house is only half-way up the hill; we had another three thousand feet or so before we reached the summit. Slowly, on second, we addressed ourselves to the ascent. We were only a mile from the custom house, when, for the second time, we met the Alfa Romeo descending. It disappeared, carrying with it a load of hatred, envy and mixed uncharitableness of every variety.

The road mounted and mounted. We passed through the region of pine woods. Around and above us, now, the slopes were bare; quite close, among the nearer summits, across the valley, were patches of snow. For all that the season was summer, the air was uncommonly sharp and nipping. A wind blew; in the shade it was positively cold. But that did not prevent the car from boiling.

The hospice and the hotels of the Mont Cenis stand on the shores of a lake in the middle of a little plateau that lies, a miracle of flatness, amid the surrounding perpendicularity. Towards the Italian side this shelf among the hills ends abruptly in what is nearly a precipice. For the last four or five hundred feet the road leading up to it is terraced out of the rock and rises with uncommon steepness. We were half-way up these final zigzags, when all at once, bursting with a roar round the corner of a bluff that had muffled the sound of its approach, the scarlet Alfa Romeo appeared at the bottom of the precipice up which we were painfully zig-zagging. It came up after us, like a wild beast pursuing its prey, bellowing. Just as we reached the top, the monster overhauled us, passed and went racing across the plain. Our humiliation was complete. Envy and discontent boiled up within us, like the water boiling in the radiator of our miserable little machine. "If only," we said, "if only we had a real car. . . ." We longed to ex-change the passion of envy for the equally malignant and un-Christian passions of pride and contempt, to be those who pass exul-tantly instead of those who are passed. "Yea, also the heart of the sons of men is full of evil, and madness is in their heart while they live, and after that they go to the dead." When we reached the hotel, the Alfa Romeo had turned round and was just preparing to begin its third descent. "It's an ugly-looking car," we said.

Such are the moral consequences of being the owner of a small car. We tried to reason with ourselves. "After all," we said, "this little machine has done good service. It has taken us over bad roads, up and down enormous hills, through a variety of countries. It has taken us, not merely through space, across the face of the map, but through time—from epoch to epoch—through art, through many languages and customs, through philology and anthropology. It has been the instrument of great and varied pleasures. It costs little, behaves well, its habits are as regular as those of Immanuel Kant. In its unpretentious way it is a model of virtue." All this we said, and much more; and it was comforting. But in the bottom of our hearts envy and discontent still lurked, like coiled serpents, ready to raise their heads the very next time that forty horses should pass us on a hill.

It may be objected that the small car-owner is not alone in envying. The Wander-Birds doing their four miles an hour, sweating, up the dusty hill, must envy indiscriminately both the ten and the forty horse power man. True, some of them probably do. But it must not be forgotten that there are pedestrians who walk because they genuinely prefer walking to being carried effortlessly along by a machine. In my youth I used to try to pretend that I preferred walking to other means of locomotion. But I soon found that it was not true. For a little time I was one of those hypocrites of

country heartiness (and they are quite numerous) who tramp and drink ale in little
inns, because it is the right thing to do. In
the end, however, I frankly admitted to myself and to other people that I was not one
of nature's walkers, that I did not like hearty
exercise and discomfort, and did not mean
any longer to pretend that I did. But I still
have the greatest respect for those who do,
and I consider that they are probably a superior type of humanity to the idle and com-
fort-loving breed predominant at the present
time. One of the great charms of mechanical progress is that it allows us to do everything quickly, easily and comfortably. This
is very agreeable; but I doubt whether it is,
morally speaking, very healthy. It is not
even very healthy for the body. It is in the
civilized countries, where human beings eat
most and take least exercise, that cancer is
most prevalent. The disease spreads with
every fresh expansion of Henry Ford's factories.

None the less I prefer to follow in the car.
To the Wander-Birds whom we pass on our
way, I take off my hat. It is a mark of my
sincere esteem. But inwardly I repeat to
myself the words of the Abbot in the *Canterbury Tales:* "Let Austin have his swink to
him reserved."

THE TRAVELLER'S-EYE VIEW

I COULD give many excellent reasons for my dislike of large dinner-parties, soirées, crushes, routs, conversazioni and balls. Life is not long enough and they waste precious time; the game is not worth the candle. Casual social intercourse is like dram-drinking, a mere stimulant that whips the nerves but does not nourish. And so on. These are respectable contentions and all quite true. And they have certainly had weight with me. But the final argument against large assemblages and in favour of solitude and the small intimate gathering has been, in my case, of a more personal character. It has appealed, not to my reason, but my vanity. The fact is that I do not shine in large assemblies; indeed, I scarcely glimmer. And to be dim and conscious of one's dimness is humiliating.

This incapacity to be bright in company is due entirely to my excessive curiosity. I cannot listen to what my interlocutor is saying or think of anything to say in answer to him, because I cannot help listening to the conversations being carried on by everybody else within earshot. My interlocutor, for example, is saying something very intelligent about Henry James and is obviously expecting me, when he has done, to make some smart or subtle comment. But the two women on my left are telling scandalous stories about a person I know. The man with the loud voice at the other side of the room is discussing the merits of different motor cars. The science student by the fireplace is talking about the quantum theory. The distinguished Irish lawyer is telling anecdotes in his inimitable professional manner. Behind me a youth and maiden are exchanging views on love, while from the group in the far corner I hear an occasional phrase which tells me that they are talking politics. An invincible curiosity possesses me, I long to hear exactly what each is saying. Scandal, motors, quanta, Irish bulls, love and politics seem to me incomparably more interesting than Henry James; and each of these is at the same time more interesting than all the others. Inquisitiveness flutters hopelessly this way and that, like a bird in a glass house. And the net result is that, not hearing what he says and being too much distracted to answer coherently, I make myself appear an idiot to my interlocutor, while the very number of my illicit curiosities renders it impossible for me to satisfy any single one of them.

But this excessive and promiscuous inquisitiveness, so fatal to a man who desires to mix in society, is a valuable asset to the one who merely looks on, without participating in the actions of his fellows.

For the traveller, who is compelled, whether he likes it or not, to pose as the detached onlooker, inquisitiveness is nothing less than a necessity. "Ennui," says Baudelaire, "is *fruit de la morne incuriosité.*" The tourist who has no curiosity is doomed to boredom.

There are few pleasanter diversions than to sit in cafés or restaurants or the third class carriages of railway trains, looking at one's neighbours and listening (without attempting to enter into conversation) to such scraps of their talk as are wafted across the intervening space. From their appearance, from what they say, one reconstructs in the imagination the whole character, the complete life history. Given the single fossil bone, one fancifully builds up the whole diplodocus. It is an excellent game. But it must be played discreetly. Too open a curiosity is apt to be resented. One must look and listen without appearing to be aware of anything. If the game is played by two people, comments should always be made in some language other than that of the country in which the game is played. But perhaps the most important rule of the game is that which forbids one, except in the most extraordinary cases, to make any effort to get to know the objects of one's curiosity.

For, alas, the objects of one's curiosity prove, once one has made their acquaintance, to be, almost invariably, quite unworthy of any further interest. It is possible at a distance to feel the most lively curiosity about a season ticket holder from Surbiton. His bald head is so shiny; he has such a funny waxed moustache; he gets so red in the face when he talks to his friends about the socialists; he laughs with such loud unpleasant gusto when one of them tells a dirty story; he sweats so profusely when it is hot; he holds forth so knowledgeably about roses; and his sister lives at Birmingham; his son has just won a prize for mathematics at school. At long range all this is fascinating; it stimulates the imagination. One loves the little man; he is wonderful, charming, a real slice of life. But make his acquaintance. . . . From that day forth you take pains to travel in another compartment.

How delightful, how queer and fantastic people are, at a distance! When I think of

the number of fascinating men and women
I have never known (only seen and momen-
tarily listened to) I am astonished. I can
remember hundreds of them. My favourites, I am inclined to think, were those male
and female post-office clerks who lived *en
pension* at the little hotel at Ambérieu where
once I stayed for a week or so, finishing a
book. They were fascinating. There was
the oldish man, who always came in late for
dinner, wearing a cap—a grim, taciturn
fellow he was; there was the very young
boy, not at all grim, but silent out of pure
shyness; there was the very bright, lively,
meridional fellow, who made jokes all the
time and flirtatiously teased the young
ladies; and the three young ladies, one ugly
but tolerably lively, one rather pretty but
limp and chlorotic, and the third so full of
attractive vitality that she compelled one to
think her pretty—such rolling black eyes,
such a smile, such a voice, so witty! The
shy young man gazed like a calf, blushed
when she looked at him, smiled oxishly
when she talked, and forgot to eat his dinner.
Her presence thawed the grim and grizzled
man and roused the meridional to yet higher
flights. And her superiority was so enormous that the ugly girl and the chlorotic girl
were not in the least jealous, but worshipped

her. It is absurd to be jealous of the gods.

How I adored that party! With what passionate interest I overlooked them from my table in the little dining-room! How attentively I eavesdropped! I learned where they had spent their holidays, which of them had been to Paris, where their relations lived, what they thought of the post-master of Ambérieu, and a host of other things, all wonderfully interesting and exciting. But not for the world would I have made their acquaintance. The landlady offered to introduce me; but I declined the honour. I am afraid she thought me a snob; she was proud of her pensionnaires. It was impossible for me to explain that my reluctance to know them was due to the fact that I loved them even more than she did. To know them would have spoilt everything. From wonderful and mysterious beings, they would have degenerated into six rather dull and pathetic little employés, condemned to pass their lives drearily in a small provincial town.

And then there were the millionaires at Padua. How much we enjoyed those! It was the waiter who told us they were plutocrats. In the restaurant of the Hotel Storione at Padua there is one special table, it appears, reserved for millionaires. Four or five of them lunched there regularly every day while we were in the hotel. Superb figures they were and wonderfully in character, like millionaires in an Italian film. In an American film, of course, the type is very different. A Hollywood millionaire is a strong, silent man, clean-shaven, with a face, either like a hatchet or an uncooked muffin. These, on the contrary, had tremendous beards, talked a great deal, were over-dressed and wore white gloves. They looked like a little party of Bluebeards.

Another of my remembered favourites is the siren we saw at the Ristorante Centrale at Genoa. She sat at a neighbouring table with four men, all desperately in love with her, talking, one could see by the way they listened and laughed, like all the heroines of Congreve rolled into one. One of the men was a Turk and had to have recourse periodically to the interpreter, without whose aid the majority of diners in that polyglot restaurant would be unable to order their macaroni. One—he was old and paid for the dinner—must have been her husband or her lover. Poor fellow, he looked rather glum sometimes, when she addressed herself too fascinatingly to the Turk, who was her principal victim, or one of the other men. But then she gave him a smile, she lifted her pale

blue-grey eyes at him and he was happy
again. No, not happy exactly; happy is the
wrong word. Drunk—that would be more
like it, I imagine. Deliriously joyful on the
surface; and within bottomlessly miserable.
So we speculated, romantically, at long
range. What we should have discovered on
a nearer acquaintance I do not know—I do
not want to know.

The most uninteresting human being seen
at a little distance by a spectator with a
lively fancy and a determination to make
the most of life takes on a mysterious charm,
becomes odd and exciting. One can work up
a thrilling emotion about distant and unknown people—an emotion which it is impossible to recapture after personal acquaintance, but which yields place to understanding and consequent affection or antipathy.

Certain authors have exploited, either deliberately or because they could not do otherwise, their spectator's emotion in the presence of unknown actors. There is Joseph
Conrad, for example. The mysterious thrilling charm of his characters, particularly his
female characters, is due to the fact that he
knows nothing at all about them. He sits
at a distance, he watches them acting and
then wonders and wonders, through pages
of Marlow's winding narratives, why on

earth they acted as they did, what were their
motives, what they felt and thought. The
God's-eye view of those novelists who really
know, or pretend they know, exactly what
is going on in the minds of their characters,
is exchanged for the traveller's-eye view, the
view of the stranger who starts with no
knowledge whatever of the actors' personali-
ties and can only infer from their gestures
what is happening in their minds. Conrad,
it must be admitted, manages to infer very
little; he lacks the palæontologist's imagination, has little power of reconstructing
thought from seen behaviour. At the end
of a novel, his heroines are as shadowy as
they were at the beginning. They have
acted, and Conrad has lengthily wondered—
without discovering—why they have acted
in this particular way. His bewilderment is
infectious; the reader is just as hopelessly
puzzled as the author and, incidentally, finds
the characters just as wonderfully mysterious. Mystery is delightful and exciting; but
it is foolish to admire it too highly. A thing
is mysterious merely because it is unknown.
There will always be mysteries because there
will always be unknown and unknowable
things. But it is best to know what is knowable. There is no credit about not knowing
what can be known. Some literary men, for

example, positively pride themselves on their
ignorance of science; they are fools and arrogant at that.   If Conrad's characters are
mysterious, it is not because they are complicated, difficult or subtle characters, but
simply because he does not understand them;
not knowing what they are like, he speculates, unsuccessfully, and finally admits that
he finds them inscrutable.   The honesty with
which he confesses his ignorance is meritorious, not the ignorance.   The characters of
the great novelists, like Dostoievsky and
Tolstoy, are not mysterious; they are perfectly well understood and clearly displayed.
Such writers live with their creations.   Conrad only looks on from a distance, without
understanding them, without even making
up plausible hypotheses about them out of
his imagination.

He differs in this respect from Miss
Katherine Mansfield, another writer who
takes the traveller's-eye view of human
beings.   For Miss Mansfield has a lively
fancy.   Like Conrad, she sees her characters
from a distance, as though at another table
in a café: she overhears snatches of their
conversations—about their aunts in Batter-
sea, their stamp collections, their souls—and
she finds them extraordinary, charming beyond all real and knowable people, odd, im-

mensely exciting. She finds that they are
Life itself—lovely, fantastic Life. Very
rarely does she go beyond this long-range
café acquaintanceship with her personages,
rarely makes herself at home in their flat
everyday lives. But where Conrad be-
wilderedly speculates, Miss Mansfield uses
her imagination. She invents suitable lives
for the fabulous creatures glimpsed at the
café. And how thrilling those fancied lives
always are! Thrilling, but just for that
reason not very convincing. Miss Mansfield's studies of interiors are like those brilliant palæontological reconstructions one
sees in books of popular science—the
ichthyosaurus in its native waters, ptero-
dactyls fluttering and swooping in the tepid
tertiary sky—too excitingly romantic, in
spite of their air of realism, to be quite
genuine. Her characters are seen with an
extraordinary brilliance and precision, as one
sees a party of people in a lighted drawing-
room, at night, through an uncurtained window—one of those mysteriously significant
Parties in Parlours of which we read in *Peter
Bell:*

> Some sipping punch, some sipping tea,
> And all as silent as could be,
> All silent, and all damned.

One sees them for a moment, haloed with
significance. They seem fabulous (though
of course, in point of actual fact and to those
sitting in the room with them, they are nothing of the kind). Then one passes, they dis-
appear. Each of Miss Mansfield's stories is
a window into a lighted room. The glimpse
of the inhabitants sipping their tea and
punch is enormously exciting. But one
knows nothing, when one has passed, of
what they are really like. That is why,
however thrilling at a first reading, her
stories do not wear. Tchekov's do; but then
he had lived with his people as well as
looked at them through the window. The
traveller's-eye view of men and women is
not satisfying. A man might spend his life
in trains and restaurants and know nothing
of humanity at the end. To know, one must
be an actor as well as a spectator. One must
dine at home as well as in restaurants, must
give up the amusing game of peeping in at
unknown windows to live quietly, flatly, un-
excitingly indoors. Still, the game, if it is
kept as an occasional diversion and not
treated as the serious business of life, is a
very good one. And on a journey it is your
only travelling picquet.

GUIDE-BOOKS

FOR every traveller who has any taste of his own, the only useful guide-book will be the one which he himself has written. All others are an exasperation. They mark with asterisks the works of art which he finds dull, and they pass over in silence those which he admires. They make him travel long miles to see a mound of rubbish; they go into ecstasies over mere antiquity. Their practical information is invariably out of date. They recommend bad hotels and qualify good ones as "modest." In a word, they are intolerable.

How often I have cursed Baron Baedeker for sending me through the dust to see some nauseating Sodoma or drearily respectable Andrea del Sarto! How angry I have been with him for starring what is old merely because it is old! And how I have hated him for his lack of discrimination! He has a way of lumping all old things of one class together and treating them as if, being made at the same period, their merit were exactly equal. For example, the stained glass windows at Sens are treated by the guide-books as though they were just like all other stained glass of the fourteenth century, when in fact they are unique in boldness and beauty of design. Some very great artist made the series of Bible illustrations at Sens. The Baron speaks as highly of the competent craftsman's work at Chartres and Canterbury.

Similarly the monuments in the church of Brou and the choir screen at Chartres get as many stars as the tomb of Ilaria del Carretto at Lucca, or Della Robbia's bas-relief in the Opera del Duomo at Florence. They are all of them specimens of Renaissance sculpture. There is only this slight difference between them: that the Italian works happen to be consummate masterpieces, while the French are mere barbarisms—that at Brou positively and piercingly vulgar, that at Chartres well-meaning, laborious, and sincerely dull. And so totally does the Baron lack a sense of proportion that he gives as many stars to the church of Brou as to Bourges cathedral, recommending with equal enthusiasm a horrible little architectural nightmare and the grandest, the most strangely and fabulously beautiful building in Europe.

Imbecile! But a learned, and, alas, indispensable imbecile. There is no escape; one must travel in his company—at any rate on a first journey. It is only after having scrupulously done what Baedeker commands, after having discovered the Baron's lapses in taste, his artistic prejudices and antiquarian snobberies, that the tourist can compile that personal guide which is the only guide for him. If he had but possessed it on his first tour! But alas, though it is easy to take other people in by your picturesque accounts of places you have never seen, it is hard to take in yourself. The personal guide-book must be the fruit of bitter personal experience.

The only satisfactory substitute for a guide written by oneself is a guide which is copiously illustrated. To know the images of things is the next best to knowing the things themselves. Illustrations allow one to see what precisely it is that the Baron is recommending. A reproduction of those luscious Sodomas would enable one to discount the asterisks in the text. A few photographs of the tombs at Tarquinia would convince one that they were incomparably better worth looking at than the Forum. A picture of the church of Brou would excuse one from ever going near it. The best illustrated guide I know is Pampaloni's Road Book of Tuscany, in which the usual information is briefly summarized, the main routes from place to place described and nothing starred that is not reproduced in a photograph.

For some tastes, I know, Pampaloni seems a little too dry. All the cackle—even as much of it as gets into Baedeker—is cut, and one is left only with a telegraphic statement of facts and the photographs. Personally I have no great weakness for cackle (unless it be the cackle of genius) and so find Pampaloni perfectly satisfying. Many tourists, however, prefer a more literary guide. They like sentiment, and purple passages and states of soul in front of the Colosseum by moonlight, and all the rest. So do I—but not from the pens of the sort of people who write chatty guides. To me, even Baedeker seems at times rather too lyrical. I like my guides to be informative, unenthusiastic and, where practical matters are concerned, up-to-date—which Baedeker, by the way (reluctant, I suppose, for patriotic reasons to acknowledge the fact of the late War) is not. If I want cackle I take with me a better stylist than the Baron or his gushing substitutes.

The only literary guides I enjoy are the really bad ones—so bad that their badness makes, so to speak, a full circle and becomes something sublime. Your ordinary literary guides are never bad in the superlative way. Theirs is that well-bred, efficient mediocrity for which there is nothing whatever to be said. It is only in obscure local guides that one finds the sublimely ludicrous. In any town it is always worth taking a look at the local guide. If you are lucky you will find one in which a train is called "Stevenson's magic babe." Not often, I admit (for it is not every day that a genius is born who can hit on such felicities); but often enough to make the search worth while. I myself have found some notable passages in local Italian guides. This description of a sixth-rate "Venus rising from the Sea" is juicy: "*Venere, abbigliata di una calda nudità, sorge dalle onde. . . . E'una seducente figura di donna, palpitante, voluttuosa. Sembra che sotto l'epidermide pulsino le vene frementi e scorre tepido il sangue. L'occhio languido pare inviti a una dolce tregenda.*" D'Annunzio himself could hardly have done better. But the finest specimen of the guide-book style I have ever met with was in France. It is a description of Dijon. "*Comme une jolie femme dont une maturité savoureuse arrondit les formes plus pleines, la capitale de la Bourgogne a fait, en grandissant, éclater la tunique étroite de ses vieilles murailles; elle a revêtu la robe plus*

moderne et plus confortable des larges boule-
vards, des places spacieuses, des faubourgs
s'égrenant dans les jardins; mais elle a gardé
le corps aux lignes pures, aux charmants
détails que des siècles épris d'art avaient
amoureusement orné." Hats off to France!
It is with alacrity, on this occasion, that I
accede to Lord Rothermere's request.

Old guide-books, so out of date to be historical documents, make excellent travelling-
companions. An early Murray is a treasure.
Indeed, any volume of European travels,
however dull, is interesting, provided that it
be written before the age of railways and
Ruskin. It is delightful to read on the spot
the impressions and opinions of tourists who
visited a hundred years ago, in the vehicles
and with the æsthetic prejudices of the
period, the places which you are visiting
now. The voyage ceases to be a mere tour
through space; you travel through time and
thought as well. They are morally whole-
some reading too, these old books of travel;
for they make one realize the entirely accidental character of all our tastes and our
fundamental intellectual beliefs. It seems
to us axiomatic, for example, that Giotto
was a great artist; and yet Goethe, when he
went to Assisi, did not even take the trouble
to look at the frescoes in the church. For

him, the only thing worth seeing at Assisi
was the portico of the Roman temple. We
for our part cannot get much pleasure out
of Guercino; and yet Stendhal was ravished
by him. We find Canova "amusing" and
sometimes, as in the statue of Pauline Bor-
ghese, really charming in a soft, voluptuous
way (the very cushion on which she reclines
bulges out voluptuously; one is reminded of
those positively indecent clouds over which
Correggio's angels look down at one from
the dome at Parma). But we cannot quite
agree with Byron when he says "Such as the
Great of yore, Canova is to-day." And yet
after all, Goethe, Stendhal, and Byron were
no fools. Given their upbringing, they could
not have thought differently. We would
have thought just as they did, if we had
lived a hundred years ago. Our altered
standards of appreciation and generally
greater tolerance are chiefly the result of increased acquaintance with the art of every
nation and period—an acquaintance due in
its turn chiefly to photography. The vastly
greater part of the world's art has been non-
realistic; we know the world's art as our
ancestors never did; it is therefore only to
be expected that we should be much more
favourably disposed to non-realistic art,
much less impressed by realism as such than

men who were brought up almost exclusively in the knowledge of Greek, Roman and modern realism. These old books teach us not to be too arrogant and cocksure in our judgments. We too shall look foolish in our turn.

There are so many of these old books and they are all so characteristic of their epoch, that one can select them almost at random from the shelves of a well-stocked library, certain that whatever one lights on will be entertaining and instructive reading. Speaking from my own personal experience, I have always found Stendhal particularly agreeable as an Italian companion. The *Promenades dans Rome* have accompanied me on many of my walks in that city and never failed to please. Very enjoyable too, when one is in Rome, is the too much neglected Veuillot. I will not pretend that Veuillot is a great writer. Indeed, much of his charm and apparent originality consists in the merely accidental fact that his prejudices were unlike those which most travellers bring with them to Italy. We are so much accustomed to hearing that the temporal power was an unmixed evil and that the priests were the cause of Italy's degradation, that a man who tells us the contrary seems startlingly original. After the denunciations of so many Protestants and free-thinkers we read his book, if it be tolerably well written (and Veuillot was a first-rate journalist), with a special pleasure. (It is, in the same way, the unusualness of the point of view from which it is written that makes *Les Paysans* of Balzac seem an even more remarkable book than it really is. We are used to reading novels in which the humble virtues of the peasant are exalted, his hard lot deplored and the tyranny of the landlord denounced. Balzac starts with the assumption that the peasant is an unmitigated ruffian and demands our sympathy for the unhappy landlord, who is represented as suffering incessant and unmerited persecution at the hands of the peasants. Balzac's reading of social history may not be correct; but it is at least refreshingly unlike that of most novelists who deal with similar themes.) *Les Parfums de Rome* shares with *Les Paysans* the merit of being written from an unexpected point of view. Veuillot tours the papal states determined to see in them the earthly paradise. And he succeeds. His Holiness has only happy subjects. Outside this blessed fold prowl the wild beasts, Cavour, Mazzini, Garibaldi and the rest; it is the duty of every right-thinking man to see that they do not break in. This is his theme and he finds in everything he sees excuses for recurring to it. *Les Parfums de Rome* is written with a refreshing intemperance of language. Veuillot, like Zimri, was

> So over violent or over civil,
> That every man with him was God or Devil.

Moreover he was logical and had the courage of his convictions. How admirable, for example, is his denunciation of all pagan art on the ground that it is not Christian! While all the rest of the world grovel before the Greeks and Romans, Veuillot, the logical ultramontanist, condemns them and all their works, on principle, contemptuously. It is delightful.

Of the other old travelling-companions who have given me pleasure by the way I can only mention a few. There is that mine of information, the Président des Brosses. No one is a better companion on the Italian tour. Our own Young is nearly as good in France. Miss Berry's journals of travels are full of interest. There are good things to be got from Lady Mary Montagu. Beckford is the perfect dilettante. But plain Bible-selling Borrow has the credit of being the first man to appreciate El Greco.

If pictures are not your chief interest, there is the admirable Dr. Burney, whose

Musical Tours are as instructive as they are
delightful. His Italian volumes are valuable because, among many other reasons,
they make one realize what had happened,
during the eighteenth century, to all the
prodigious talent which had gone, in the
past, to painting pictures, carving statues
and building churches. It had all gone into
music. The very street players were accomplished contrapuntists; the peasants sang divinely (you should hear the way they sing
now!), every church had a good choir which
was perpetually producing new masses,
motets and oratorios; there was hardly a
lady or gentleman who was not a first-rate
amateur performer; there were innumerable
concerts. Dr. Burney found it a musician's
paradise. And what has happened to Italian
genius nowadays? Does it still exist? or is
it dead?

It still exists, I think; but it has been deflected out of music, as it was deflected out
of the visual arts, into politics and, later,
into business and engineering. The first
two-thirds of the nineteenth century were
sufficiently occupied in the achievement of
freedom and unity. The sixty years since
then have been devoted to the exploitation
of the country's resources; and such energy
as has been left over from that task has gone

into politics. One day, when they have fin-
ished putting modern comfort into the old
house, have turned out the obstreperous
servants and installed a quiet, honest house-
keeper—one day, perhaps, the Italians will
allow their energy and their talent to flow
back into the old channels. Let us hope
they will.

SPECTACLES

I NEVER move without a plentiful supply of optical glass. A pair of spectacles for reading, a pair for long range, with a couple of monocles in reserve—these go with me everywhere. To break all these, it would need an earthquake or a railway accident. And absence of mind would have to be carried to idiocy before they could all be lost. Moreover, there is a further safety in a numerous supply: for matter, who can doubt it? is not neutral, as the men of science falsely teach, but slightly malignant, on the side of the devils against us. This being so, one pair of spectacles must inevitably break or lose itself, just when you can least afford to do without and are least able to replace it. But inanimate matter, so called, is no fool; and when a pair of spectacles realizes that you carry two or three other pairs in your pockets and suit-cases, it will understand that the game is hopeless and, so far from deliberately smashing or losing itself, will take pains to remain intact.

But when, in any month after the vernal equinox and before the autumn, my wanderings take me southwards, towards the sun, my armoury of spectacles is enlarged by the addition of three pairs of coloured glasses—two of lighter and darker shades of green, and one black. The glare from dusty roads, from white walls and the metallic, blue-hot sky is painful and even dangerous. As the summer advances or retreats, as the light of each day waxes or declines, I adjust to my nose the pale green, the dark green or the black spectacles. In this way I am able to temper the illumination of the world to my exact requirements.

But even if I suffered not at all from excess of light and could perform without winking the feats of the eagle and the oxy-acetylene welder, I should still take coloured glasses with me on my southward travels. For they have an æsthetic as well as a merely practical use. They improve the landscape as well as soothe the eyes.

As one approaches the great desert belt which bands the earth with some thousand miles of aridity to this side of the tropic of Cancer, the landscape suffers a change which to us northerners at least seems a change for the worse. It loses its luxuriant greenness. South of Lyons (except among the mountains and in the marshes) there is no grass worthy of the name. The deciduous trees grow with reluctance, yielding place to the

black cypress and pine, the dark green laurel
ar 1 juniper, the pale grey olive. The greens
in an Italian landscape are either pale and
dusty or glossily dark. Only when you
climb to two thousand feet—and by no
means invariably then—does anything like
the brilliant, the seemingly self-luminous
verdure of the English scene appear. The
typical north Italian landscape is one of
hills, the lower slopes grey with olives, the
summits, when they are above the level of
cultivation, bare and brown. It is a landscape that makes a not entirely satisfactory
compromise between the northern type and
the fully southern. The English scene is
made rich and comfortable by the bosomy
forms and the damply glowing colours of its
luxuriant foliage. And its rather rotund
earthiness is tempered and made romantic by
the bloom of mist that half veils it from
sight. The southern, Mediterranean landscape, which makes its first Italian appearance at Terracina, is bare, sharp-outlined and
austerely brilliant. The air is clear, and the
far-seen earth seems itself to be made of
coloured air. The landscape of northern
Italy is neither northern nor southern—
neither aerially bright and light nor, on the
other hand, rounded and softly, luxuriously
green.

It is here, in this half-parched landscape that is not yet refined to a bright asceticism, that the judicious traveller will don his green spectacles. The effect is magical. Every blade of dusty grass becomes on the instant rich with juicy life. Whatever greenness lurks in the grey of the olive trees shines out, intensified. The dried-up woods reburgeon. The vines and the growing corn seem to have drunk of a refreshing rain. All that the scene lacked to make it perfectly beautiful is instantaneously added. Through green spectacles, it becomes the northern landscape, but transformed and glorified— brighter, more nobly dramatic and romantic.

Green spectacles make excellent wearing, too, on the shores of the northern Mediterranean. In the south the blue of the sea is beautifully dark, like lapis-lazuli. It is the wine-dark sea of antiquity in contrast with which the sunlit land seems more than ever light, clear-coloured and aerial. But north of Rome the blue is insufficiently intense; it is a china not a lazuline blue. The sea at Monaco and Genoa, at Spezia and Civitavecchia has the blue, glassy stare of a doll's eye —a stare that becomes very soon enraging in its enormous blankness and brightness. Put on green spectacles and this blank stare becomes at once the darkly glaucous, enigmatic gaze that shines up, between the cypresses, from the pools in the Villa d'Este gardens at Tivoli. From imbecile, the sea turns siren, and the arid hills that overhang it break into verdure as though beneath the feet of the spring.

Or if you like, you may put on black spectacles and so deepen the colour till it approaches that of the wine-dark Mediterranean of Greece and Magna Græcia and the isles. Black spectacles do nothing, however, to make the land more southern in aspect. By the side of their dark sea, the southern coasts seem built of bright air. Black spectacles may darken the northern sea; but they also give weight and an added solidity to the land. The glass which shall make the world seem brighter, clearer and lighter, put sunlight into the grey landscape and turn north into south still, alas, remains to be invented.

THE COUNTRY

IT is a curious fact, of which I can think of no satisfactory explanation, that enthusiasm for country life and love of natural scenery are strongest and most widely diffused precisely in those European countries which have the worst climate and where the search for the picturesque involves the greatest discomfort. Nature worship increases in an exact ratio with distance from the Mediterranean. The Italians and the Spanish have next to no interest in nature for its own sake. The French feel a certain affection for the country, but not enough to make them desire to live in it if they can possibly inhabit the town. The south Germans and Swiss form an apparent exception to the rule. They live nearer to the Mediterranean than the Parisians, and yet they are fonder of the country. But the exception, as I have said, is only apparent; for owing to their remoteness from the ocean and the mountainous conformation of the land, these people enjoy for a large part of each year a climate that is, to all intents, arctic. In England, where the climate is detestable, we

love the country so much that we are prepared, for the privilege of living in it, to
get up at seven, summer and winter, bicycle,
wet or fine, to a distant station and make an
hour's journey to our place of labour. In
our spare moments we go for walking tours,
and we regard caravanning as a pleasure.
In Holland the climate is far more unpleasant than in England and we should consequently expect the Dutch to be even keener
country-fanciers than ourselves. The ubiqui-
tous water makes it difficult, however, for
season ticket holders to settle down casually
in the Dutch country-side. But if unsuitable
as building land, the soggy meadows of the
Low Countries are firm enough to carry tents.
Unable to live permanently in the country,
the Dutch are the greatest campers in the
world. Poor Uncle Toby, when he was
campaigning in those parts, found the damp
so penetrating, that he was forced to burn
good brandy in his tent to dry the air. But
then my Uncle Toby was a mere English-
man, brought up in a climate which, compared with that of Holland, is balmy. The
hardier Dutch camp out for pleasure. Of
Northern Germany it is enough to say that
it is the home of the Wander-Birds. And as
for Scandinavia—it is well known that there
is no part of the world, excluding the tropics,

where people so freely divest themselves of their clothing. The Swedish passion for nature is so strong that it can only be adequately expressed when in a state of nature. "As souls unbodied," says Donne, "bodies unclothed must be to taste whole joys." Noble, nude and far more modern than any other people in Europe, they sport in the icy waters of the Baltic, they roam naked in the primeval forest. The cautious Italian, meanwhile, bathes in his tepid sea during only two months out of the twelve; always wears a vest under his shirt and never leaves the town, if he can possibly help it, except when the summer is at its most hellish, and again, for a little while, in the autumn, to superintend the making of his wine.

Strange and inexplicable state of affairs! Is it that the dwellers under inclement skies are trying to bluff themselves into a belief that they inhabit Eden? Do they deliberately love nature in the hope of persuading themselves that she is as beautiful in the damp and darkness as in the sunlight? Do they brave the discomforts of northern country life in order to be able to say to those who live in more favoured lands: You see, our countryside is just as delightful as yours; and the proof is that we live in it!

But whatever the reason, the fact remains

that nature worship does increase with distance from the sun. To search for causes is hopeless; but it is easy and at the same time not uninteresting to catalogue effects. Thus, our Anglo-Saxon passion for the country has had the result of turning the country into one vast town; but a town without the urban conveniences which make tolerable life in a city. For we all love the country so much, that we desire to live in it, if only during the night, when we are not at work. We build cottages, buy season tickets and bicycles to take us to the station. And meanwhile the country perishes. The Surrey I knew as a boy was full of wildernesses. To-day Hindhead is hardly distinguishable from the Elephant and Castle. Mr. Lloyd George has built a week-end cottage (not, one feels, without a certain appositeness) at the foot of the Devil's Jumps; and several thousand people are busily following his example. Every lane is now a street. Harrod's and Selfridge's call daily. There is no more country, at any rate within fifty miles of London. Our love has killed it.

Except in summer, when it is too hot to stay in town, the French, and still more, the Italians, do not like the country. The result is that they still have country not to like. Solitude stretches almost to the gates of

Paris. (And Paris, remember, still has gates; you drive up to them along country roads, enter and find yourself within a few minutes of the centre of the city). The silence sleeps unbroken, except by the faint music of ghosts, within a mile of the Victor Emanuel monument at Rome.

In France, in Italy none but countrymen live in the country. Agriculture there is taken seriously; farms are still farms and not week-end cottages; and the corn is still permitted to grow on what, in England, would be desirable building land.

In Italy, despite the fact that the educated Italians like the country still less than the French, there are fewer complete solitudes than in France, because there are more countrymen. And how few there are in France! A drive from the Belgian frontier to the Mediterranean puts life and meaning into those statistics from which we learn, academically and in theory, that France is under-populated. Long stretches of open road extend between town and town.

> Like stones of worth they thinly placed are,
> Or captain jewels in the carcanet.

Even the villages are few and far between. And those innumerable farms which shine out from among the olive trees on Italian hill-sides—one looks in vain for their French counterpart. Driving through the fertile plains of Central France, one can turn one's eyes over the fields and scarcely see a house. And then, what forests still grow on French soil! Huge tracts of uninhabited woodland, with not a week-ender or a walking-tourist to be seen within their shades.

This state of things is delightful to me personally; for I like the country, enjoy solitude, and take no interest in the political future of France. But to a French patriot I can imagine that a drive across his native land must seem depressing. Huge populations, upon whose skulls the bump of philoprogenitiveness can be seen at a quarter of a mile, pullulate on the further side of almost every frontier. Without haste, without rest, as though by a steadily continued miracle, the Germans and the Italians multiply themselves, like loaves and fishes. Every three years a million brand new Teutons peer across the Rhine, a million Italians are wondering where they are going to find room, in their narrow country, to live. And there are no more Frenchmen. Twenty years hence, what will happen? The French Government offers prizes to those who produce large families. In vain; everybody knows all about birth control and even in the least educated classes there are no prejudices and a great deal of thrift. Hordes of black-amoors are drilled and armed; but black-amoors can be but a poor defence, in the long run, against European philoprogenitive-ness. Sooner or later, this half-empty land will be colonized. It may be done peace-fully, it may be done with violence; let us hope peacefully, with the consent and at the invitation of the French themselves. Already the French import, temporarily, I forget how many foreign labourers every year. In time, no doubt, the foreigners will begin to settle: the Italians in the south, the Germans in the east, the Belgians in the north, perhaps even a few English in the west.

Frenchmen may not like the plan; but until all nations agree to practise birth con-trol to exactly the same extent, it is the best that can be devised.

The Portuguese who, in the later sixteenth and seventeenth century, suffered acutely from under-population (half the able-bodied men had emigrated to the colonies, where they died in war or of tropical diseases, while those who stayed at home were periodically decimated by famine—for the colonies pro-duced only gold, not bread) solved their problem by importing negro slaves to work the deserted fields. The negroes settled. They intermarried with the inhabitants. In two or three generations the race which had conquered half the world was extinct, and Portugal, with the exception of a small area in the north, was inhabited by a hybrid race of Eur-Africans. The French may think themselves lucky if, avoiding war, they can fill their depleted country with civilized white men.

Meanwhile, the emptiness of France is a delight to all lovers of nature and solitude. But even in Italy, where farms and peasants and peasants' children are thick on the land, the lover of the country feels much happier than he does in what may actually be more sparsely inhabited districts of the home counties. For farms and peasants are country products, as truly native to the land as trees or growing corn, and as inoffensive. It is the urban interloper who ruins the English country. Neither he nor his house belong to it. In Italy, on the other hand, when the rare trespasser from the town does venture into the country, he finds it genuinely rustic. The country is densely populated, but it is still the country. It has not been killed by the deadly kindness of those who, like myself, are nature's townsmen.

The time is not far distant, I am afraid,

when every countryside in Europe, even the Spanish, will be invaded by nature lovers from the towns. It is not so long ago, after all, since Evelyn was horrified and disgusted by the spectacle of the rocks at Clifton. Till the end of the eighteenth century every sensible man, even in England, even in Sweden, feared and detested mountains. The modern enthusiasm for wild nature is a recent growth and began—along with kindness to animals, industrialism and railway travelling— among the English. (It is, perhaps, not surprising that the people which first made its cities uninhabitable with dirt, noise and smoke should also have been the first to love nature.) From this island, country sentiment has spread with machinery. All the world welcomed machinery with delight; but country sentiment has so far flourished only in the north. Still, there are evident signs that even the Latins are becoming infected by it. In France and Italy wild nature has become—though to a far less extent than in England—the object of *snobisme*. It is rather chic, in those countries, to be fond of nature. In a few years, I repeat, everybody will adore it as a matter of course. For even in the north those who do not in the least like the country are made to imagine that they do by the artful and never-ceasing suggestions of the people whose interest it is that the country should be liked. No modern man, even if he loathed the country, could resist the appeal of the innumerable advertisements, published by railways, motor car manufacturers, thermos flask makers, sporting tailors, house agents and all the rest whose livelihood depends on his frequently visiting the country. Now the art of advertising in the Latin countries is still poorly developed. But it is improving even there. The march of progress is irresistible. Fiat and the State Railways have only to hire American advertising managers to turn the Italians into a race of week-enders and season ticket holders. Already there is a *Città Giardino* on the outskirts of Rome; Ostia is being developed as a residential seaside suburb; the recently opened motor road has placed the Lakes at the mercy of Milan. My grandchildren, I foresee, will have to take their holidays in Central Asia.

BOOKS FOR THE JOURNEY

ALL tourists cherish an illusion, of which no amount of experience can ever completely cure them; they imagine that they will find time, in the course of their travels, to do a lot of reading. They see themselves, at the end of a day's sightseeing or motoring, or while they are sitting in the train, studiously turning over the pages of all the vast and serious works which, at ordinary seasons, they never find time to read. They start for a fortnight's tour in France, taking with them *The Critique of Pure Reason*, *Appearance and Reality*, the complete works of Dante and the *Golden Bough*. They come home to make the discovery that they have read something less than half a chapter of the *Golden Bough* and the first fifty-two lines of the *Inferno*. But that does not prevent them from taking just as many books the next time they set out on their travels.

Long experience has taught me to reduce in some slight measure the dimensions of my travelling library. But even now I am far too optimistic about my powers of reading while on a journey. Along with the books which I know it is possible to read, I still continue to put in a few impossible volumes in the pious hope that some day, somehow, they will get read. Thick tomes have travelled with me for thousands of kilometres across the face of Europe and have returned with their secrets unviolated. But whereas in the past I took nothing but thick tomes, and a great quantity of them at that, I now take only one or two and for the rest pack only the sort of books which I know by experience can be read in a hotel bedroom after a day's sightseeing.

The qualities essential in a good travelling-book are these. It should be a work of such a kind that one can open it anywhere and be sure of finding something interesting, complete in itself and susceptible of being read in a short time. A book requiring continuous attention and prolonged mental effort is useless on a voyage; for leisure, when one travels, is brief and tinged with physical fatigue, the mind distracted and unapt to make protracted exertions.

Few travelling-books are better than a good anthology of poetry in which every page contains something complete and perfect in itself. The brief respites from labour which the self-immolated tourist allows himself cannot be more delightfully filled than with the reading of poetry, which may even be got by heart; for the mind, though reluctant to follow an argument, takes pleasure in the slight labour of committing melodious words to memory.

In the choice of anthologies every traveller must please himself. My own favourite is Edward Thomas's *Pocket Book of Poems and Songs for the Open Air*. Thomas was a man of wide reading and of exquisite taste, and peculiarly gifted, moreover, to be an anthologist of the Open Air. For out of the huge tribe of modern versifiers who have babbled of green fields, Thomas is almost the only one whom one feels to be a "nature poet" (the expression is somehow rather horrible, but there is no other) by right of birth and the conquest of real sympathy and understanding. It is not every one who says Lord, Lord, that shall enter into the kingdom of heaven; and few, very few of those who cry Cuckoo, Cuckoo, shall be admitted into the company of nature poets. For proof of this I refer my readers to the various volumes of Georgian poetry.

Equally well adapted, with poetry, to the traveller's need, are collections of aphorisms or maxims. If they are good—and they must be very good indeed; for there is nothing more dismal than a "Great Thought"

enunciated by an author who has not himself the elements of greatness—maxims
make the best of all reading. They take a
minute to read and provide matter upon
which thought can ruminate for hours.
None are to be preferred to La Rochefoucauld's. Myself, I always reserve my
upper left-hand waistcoat pocket for a small
sexto-decimo reprint of the *Maximes*. It is
a book to which there is no bottom or end.
For with every month that one lives, with
every accession to one's knowledge, both of
oneself and of others, it means something
more. For La Rochefoucauld knew almost
everything about the human soul, so that
practically every discovery one can make
oneself, as one advances through life, has
been anticipated by him and formulated in
the briefest and most elegant phrases. I
say advisedly that La Rochefoucauld knew
"almost" everything about the human soul;
for it is obvious that he did not know all.
He knew everything about the souls of human beings in so far as they are social animals. Of the soul of man in solitude—of
man when he is no more interested in the
social pleasures and successes which were, to
La Rochefoucauld, so all-important—he
knows little or nothing. If we desire to
know something about the human soul in

solitude—in its relations, not to man, but to God—we must go elsewhere: to the Gospels, to the novels of Dostoievsky, for example. But man in his social relationships has never been more accurately described, and his motives never more delicately analysed than by La Rochefoucauld. The aphorisms vary considerably in value; but the best of them—and their number is surprisingly large—are astonishingly profound and pregnant. They resume a vast experience. In a sentence La Rochefoucauld compresses as much material as would serve a novelist for a long story. Conversely, it would not surprise me to learn that many novelists turn to the *Maximes* for suggestions for plots and characters. It is impossible, for example, to read Proust without being reminded of the *Maximes*, or the *Maximes* without being reminded of Proust. "*Le plaisir de l'amour est d'aimer, et l'on est plus heureux par la passion que l'on a que par celle que l'on donne.*" "*Il y a des gens si remplis d'eux-mêmes, que, lorsqu'ils sont amoureux, ils trouvent moyen d'être occupés de leur passion sans l'être de la personne qu'ils aiment.*" What are all the love stories in *A la Recherche du Temps Perdu* but enormous amplifications of these aphorisms?

Proust is La Rochefoucauld magnified ten thousand times.

Hardly less satisfactory as travel books are the aphoristic works of Nietzsche. Nietzsche's sayings have this in common with La Rochefoucauld's, that they are pregnant and expansive. His best aphorisms are long trains of thought, compressed. The mind can dwell on them at length because so much is implicit in them. It is in this way that good aphorisms differ from mere epigrams, in which the whole point consists in the felicity of expression. An epigram pleases by surprising; after the first moment the effect wears off and we are no further interested in it. One is not taken in twice by the same practical joke. But an aphorism does not depend on verbal wit. Its effect is not momentary, and the more we think of it, the more substance we find in it.

Another excellent book for a journey—for it combines expansive aphorisms with anecdotes—is Boswell's *Life of Johnson* which the Oxford Press now issues, on India paper, in a single small octavo volume. (All travellers, by the way, owe much to the exertions of Henry Frowde, of the Oxford Press, the inventor, or at least the European reinventor, of that fine rag paper, impregnated with mineral matter to give it opacity, which we call India paper.) What the aphorism is to the philosophical treatise, the India paper volume is to the ponderous editions of the past. All Shakespeare, perfectly legible, gets into a volume no bigger than a single novel by the late Charles Garvice. All Pepys, or as much of him as the British public is allowed to read, can now be fitted into three pockets. And the Bible, reduced to an inch in thickness, must surely be in danger of losing those bullet-stopping qualities which it used, at any rate in romantic novels, to possess. Thanks to Henry Frowde one can get a million words of reading matter into a rucksack and hardly feel the difference in its weight.

India paper and photography have rendered possible the inclusion in a portable library of what in my opinion is the best traveller's book of all—a volume (any one of the thirty-two will do) of the twelfth, half-size edition of the *Encyclopædia Britannica*. It takes up very little room (eight and a half inches by six and a half by one is not excessive), it contains about a thousand pages and an almost countless number of curious and improbable facts. It can be dipped into anywhere, its component chapters are complete in themselves and not too long. For the traveller, disposing as he does only of brief half-hours, it is the perfect book, the more so, since I take it that, being a born traveller, he is likely also to be one of those desultory and self-indulgent readers to whom the *Encyclopædia*, when not used for some practical purpose, must specially appeal. I never pass a day away from home without taking a volume with me. It is the book of books. Turning over its pages, rummaging among the stores of fantastically varied facts which the hazards of alphabetical arrangement bring together, I wallow in my mental vice. A stray volume of the *Encyclopædia* is like the mind of a learned madman—stored with correct ideas, between which, however, there is no other connection than the fact that there is a B in both. From orach, or mountain spinach, one passes direct to oracles. That one does not oneself go mad, or become, in the process of reading the *Encyclopædia*, a mine of useless and unrelated knowledge is due to the fact that one forgets. The mind has a vast capacity for oblivion. Providentially; otherwise, in the chaos of futile memories, it would be impossible to remember anything useful or coherent. In practice, we work with generalizations, abstracted out of the turmoil of realities. If we remembered everything perfectly we should never be able to generalize at all; for there would appear before our minds nothing but individual images, precise and different. Without ignorance we could not generalize. Let us thank Heaven for our powers of forgetting. With regard to the *Encyclopædia*, they are enormous. The mind only remembers that of which it has some need. Five minutes after reading about mountain spinach, the ordinary man, who is neither a botanist nor a cook, has forgotten all about it. Read for amusement, the *Encyclopædia* serves only to distract for the moment; it does not instruct, it deposits nothing on the surface of the mind that will remain. It is a mere time-killer and momentary tickler of the mind. I only use it for amusement on my travels; I should be ashamed to indulge so wantonly in mere curiosity at home, during seasons of serious business.

Part II: Places

MONTESENARIO

IT was March and the snow was melting. Half wintry, half vernal, the mountain looked patchy, like a mangy dog. The southward slopes were bare; but in every hollow, on the sunless side of every tree, the snow still lay, white under the blue transparent shadows.

We walked through a little pine wood; the afternoon sunlight breaking through the dark foliage lit up here a branch, there a length of trunk, turning the ruddy bark into a kind of golden coral. Beyond the wood the hill lay bare to the summit. On the very crest a mass of buildings lifted their high sunlit walls against the pale sky, a chilly little New Jerusalem. It was the monastery of Montesenario. We climbed towards it, toilsomely; for the last stage in the pilgrim's progress from Florence to Montesenario is uncommonly steep and the motor must be left behind. And suddenly, as though to welcome us, as though to encourage our efforts, the heavenly city disgorged a troop of angels. Turning a corner of the track we saw them coming down to meet us, by two and two in a long file; angels in black cassocks with round black hats on their heads —a seminary taking its afternoon airing. They were young boys, the eldest sixteen or seventeen, the youngest not more than ten. Flapping along in their black skirts they walked with an unnatural decorum. It was difficult to believe, when one saw the little fellows at the head of the crocodile, with the tall Father in charge striding along at their side, it was difficult to believe that they were not masquerading. It seemed a piece of irreverent fun; a caricature by Goya come to life. But their faces were serious; chubby or adolescently thin, they wore already an unctuously clerical expression. It was no joke. Looking at those black-robed children, one wished that it had been.

We climbed on; the little priestlings descended out of sight. And now at last we were at the gates of the heavenly city. A little paved and parapeted platform served as landing to the flight of steps that led up into the heart of the convent. In the middle of the platform stood a more than life-sized statue of some unheard-of saint. It was a comically admirable piece of eighteenth-century baroque. Carved with coarse brilliance, the creature gesticulated ecstatically, rolling its eyes to heaven; its garments flapped around it in broad folds. It was not, somehow, the sort of saint one expected to see standing sentinel over the bleakest hermitage in Tuscany. And the convent itself—that too seemed incongruous on the top of this icy mountain. For the heavenly city was a handsome early baroque affair with *sette-cento* trimmings and additions. The church was full of twiddly gilt carvings and dreadfully competent pictures; the remains of the seven pious Florentines who, in the thirteenth century, fled from the city of destruction in the plain below, and founded this hermitage on the mountain, were coffered in a large gold and crystal box, illuminated, like a show-case in the drawing-room of a collector of porcelain, by concealed electric lights. No, the buildings were ludicrous. But after all, what do buildings matter? A man can paint beautiful pictures in a slum, can write poetry in Wigan; and conversely he can live in an exquisite house, surrounded by masterpieces of ancient art, and yet (as one sees almost invariably when collectors of the antique, relying for once on their own judgment, and not on tradition, "go in for" modern art) be crassly insensitive and utterly without taste. Within certain limits, environment counts for very little; it is only when environment is extremely unfavourable that it can blast or distort the powers of the mind. And however favourable, it can do nothing to extend the limits set by nature to a man's ability. So here the architecture seemed impossibly incongruous with the bleak place, with the very notion of a hermitage; but the hermits who lived in the midst of it were probably not even aware of its existence. In the shade of the absurd statue of San Filippo Benizi a Buddha would be able to think as Buddhistically as beneath the bo-tree.

In the grounds of the monastery we saw half a dozen black-frocked Servites sawing wood—sawing with vigour and humility, in spite of the twiddly gilding in the church and the *settecento* bell tower. They looked the genuine article. And the view from the mountain's second peak was in the grandest eremitic tradition. The hills stretched away as far as the eye could reach into the wintry haze, like a vast heaving sea frozen to stillness. The valleys were filled with blue shadow, and all the sunward slopes were the colour of rusty gold. At our feet the ground fell away into an immense blue gulf. The gauzy air softened every outline, smoothed away every detail, leaving only golden lights and violet shadows floating like the disembodied essence of a landscape, under the pale sky.

We stood for a long time looking out over that kingdom of silence and solemn beauty. The solitude was as profound as the shadowy gulf beneath us; it stretched to the misty horizons and up into the topless sky. Here at the heart of it, I thought, a man might begin to understand something about that part of his being which does not reveal itself in the quotidian commerce of life; which the social contacts do not draw forth, spark-like, from the sleeping flint that is an untried spirit; that part of him, of whose very existence he is only made aware in solitude and silence. And if there happens to be no silence in his life, if he is never solitary, then he may go down to his grave without a knowledge of its existence, much less an understanding of its nature or realisation of its potentialities.

We retraced our steps to the monastery and thence walked down the steep path to the motor. A mile further down the road towards Pratolino, we met the priestlings returning from their walk. Poor children! But was their lot worse, I wondered, than that of the inhabitants of the city in the valley? On their mountain top they lived under a tyrannous rule, they were taught to believe in a number of things manifestly silly. But was the rule any more tyrannous than that of the imbecile conventions which control the lives of social beings in the plain? Was snobbery about duchesses and distinguished novelists more reasonable than snobbery about Jesus Christ and the Saints? Was hard work to the greater glory of God more detestable than eight hours a day in an office for the greater enrichment of the Jews? Temperance was a bore, no doubt; but was it so nauseatingly wearisome as excess? And the expense of spirit in prayer and meditation—was that so much less amusing than the expense of spirit in a waste of shame? Driving down towards the city in the plain, I wondered. And when, in the Via Tornabuoni, we passed Mrs. Thingumy, that pillar of Anglo-American-Florentine society, in the act of laboriously squeezing herself out on to the pavement through the door of her gigantic limousine, I suddenly and perfectly understood what it was that had made those seven rich Florentine merchants, seven hundred years ago, abandon their position in the world, and had sent them up into the high wilderness, to live in holes at the tops of Montesenario. I looked back; Mrs. Thingumy was waddling across the pavement into the jeweller's shop. Yes, I perfectly understood.

PATINIR'S RIVER

THE river flows in a narrow valley between hills. A broad, a brimming and
a shining river. The hills are steep and all
of a height. Where the river bends, the hills
on one side jut forward in a bastion, the
hills on the other retreat. There are cliffs,
there are hanging woods, dark with foliage.
The sky is pale above this strip of fantastically carved and scalloped earth. A pale
sky from which it must sometimes rain
Chinese white. For there is an ashen pallor
over the rocks; and the green of the grass
and the trees is tinged with white till it has
taken on the colour of the "Emerald Green"
of children's paint-boxes.

Brimming and shining river, pale crags,
and trees richly dark, slopes where the turf
is the colour of whitened verdigris—I took
these things for fancies. Peering into the
little pictures, each painted with a million
tiny strokes of a four-haired sable brush, I
laughed with pleasure at the beauty of the
charming invention. This Joachim Patinir,
I thought, imagines delicately. For years I
was accustomed to float along that crag-

reflecting river as down a river of the mind, out of the world.

And then one day—one wet day in autumn—driving out of Namur towards Dinant through the rain, suddenly I found myself rolling, as fast as ten horses ventured to take me through the slippery mud, along the bank of this imaginary stream. The rain, it is true, a little blurred the scene. Greyly it hung, like a dirty glass, between the picture and the beholder's eye. But through it, unmistakably, I distinguished the fabulous landscape of the Fleming's little paintings. Crags, river, emerald green slopes, dark woods were there, indubitably real. I had given to Joachim Patinir the credit that was due to God. What I had taken for his exquisite invention was the real and actual Meuse.

Mile after mile we drove, from Namur to Dinant; from Dinant, mile after mile, to Givet. And it was Patinir all the way; winding river, the double line of jutting and re-entrant hill, verdigris grass, cliffs and pensile trees all the way. At Givet we left the river; for our destination was Reims and our road led us through Rethel. We left the river, but left it with the impression that it wound back, Patinir landscape after Patinir landscape, all the way to its distant source at Poissy. I should like to think, indeed, that it did. For Patinir was a charming painter and his surviving works are few. Two hundred miles of him would not be at all too much.

PORTOFERRAIO

THE sky was Tiepolo's palette. A cloud
of smoke mounted into the blue, white
where it looked towards the sun and darken-
ing, through the colour of the shadowed folds
in a wedding gown, to grey. In the foreground on the right a tall pink house went
up, glowing like a geranium, into the sunlight. There was the stuff there for a Madonna with attendant saints and angels; or
a scene from Trojan history; or a Crucifixion; or one of the little amours of Jupiter
Tonans.

The earth was Mediterranean—a piece
of the Riviera completely surrounded by
water. In a word, Elba. The hills dived
down into a handsomely curved bay, full of
bright, staring blue sea. On the headland
at one end of the bay Portoferraio was piled
up in tiers of painted stucco. At its feet lay
a little harbour bristling with masts. A
smell of fish and the memory of Napoleon
haunted the atmosphere inveterately. Conscience and Baron Baedeker had told us that
we ought to visit Napoleon's house—now,
very suitably, a natural history museum.

But we had hardened our hearts and would not go. It is very unpleasant not to have done one's duty. "How tedious is a guilty conscience," says the Cardinal in the *Duchess of Malfi*. He was quite right. We had walked the blazing streets groaning under conviction of sin.

And then, passing through a gateway in the walls of the old town, we found ourselves confronted by a scene that entirely relieved us of all our sense of guilt. For we were looking at something compared with which a house full of Napoleonic souvenirs was so obviously second-rate and dull that our rebellion against Baedeker ceased to be criminal and became positively meritorious.

Below us, on the further side of a blue inlet of the sea, and with the mountains behind it, lay a little piece of the Black Country. In the midst stood a group of blast furnaces with three huge chimneys rising from beside them like the bell towers of a cathedral. To the right of them were five or six more chimneys. Three huge cranes were perched at the water's edge, and an iron bridge led from the wharves inland to the furnaces. The chimneys, the cranes, the furnaces and buildings, the heap of rubbish, the very ground in this little area between the Mediterranean and the mountains—all were soot-black. Black against the sky, black against the golden-glaucous hills, blackly reflected in the shining blue water.

I should have painted the scene if I had known how. It was exceedingly beautiful. Beautiful and dramatic too. The mind delights in violent contrasts. Birmingham is frightful enough where it is, its body in Warwickshire and its sooty tentacles stretching out across the undulating land into Stafford. But set it down in Sicily or on the shores of Lago Maggiore and its frightfulness becomes at once more painfully apparent. In Warwickshire it is a full-length sermon on civilization, but one sleeps through sermons. Beside the Mediterranean it becomes the most bitingly memorable of epigrams. Moreover, the actual Birmingham of Warwickshire is too large to be taken in as a whole. This single piece of blackness between the blue sky and the blue sea was compactly symbolic. And because the sky and the grass were still visible all round it, the contest between industrialism and the natural beauties of the earth was much more vividly realized than where, as in the great towns of the north, industrialism has completely triumphed and one is not even aware of the existence of what has been conquered.

We stood for a long time, watching the

smoke from the chimneys as it mounted into the still air. White gauze; white satin, glossy or shadowed; feathery grey—Tiepolo's angels hovered; and the blue sky was the Madonna's silken robe; and the tall pink house on our right was the colour of one of those very handsome velvets to which, in the paradise of the last of the Venetians, the blest are so excusably partial.

THE PALIO AT SIENA

OUR rooms were in a tower. From the
windows one looked across the brown
tiled roofs to where, on its hill, stood the
cathedral. A hundred feet below was the
street, a narrow canyon between high
walls, perennially sunless; the voices of the
passers-by came up, reverberating, as out of
a chasm. Down there they walked always
in shadow; but in our tower we were the
last to lose the sunlight. On the hot days
it was cooler, no doubt, down in the street;
but we at least had the winds. The waves
of the air broke against our tower and flowed
past it on either side. And at evening, when
only the belfries and the domes and the highest roofs were still flushed by the declining
sun, our windows were level with the flight
of the swifts and swallows. Sunset after
sunset all through the long summer, they
wheeled and darted round our tower. There
was always a swarm of them intricately
manœuvring just outside the window. They
swerved this way and that, they dipped and
rose, they checked their headlong flight with
a flutter of their long pointed wings and

turned about within their own length. Compact, smooth and tapering, they seemed the incarnation of airy speed. And their thin, sharp, arrowy cry was speed made audible. I have sat at my window watching them tracing their intricate arabesques until I grew dizzy; till their shrill crying sounded as though from within my ears and their flying seemed a motion, incessant, swift and bewilderingly multitudinous, behind my eyes. And all the while the sun declined, the shadows climbed higher up the houses and towers, and the light with which they were tipped became more rosy. And at last the shadow had climbed to the very top and the city lay in a grey and violet twilight beneath the pale sky.

One evening, towards the end of June, as I was sitting at the window looking at the wheeling birds, I heard through the crying of the swifts the sound of a drum. I looked down into the shadowy street, but could see nothing. Rub-a-dub, dub, dub, dub—the sound grew louder and louder, and suddenly there appeared round the corner where our street bent out of sight, three personages out of a Pinturicchio fresco. They were dressed in liveries of green and yellow—yellow doublets slashed and tagged with green, parti-coloured hose and shoes, with feath-

ered caps of the same colours. Their leader
played the drum. The two who followed
carried green and yellow banners. Immediately below our tower the street opens out
a little into a tiny piazza. In this clear
space the three Pinturicchio figures came to
a halt and the crowd of little boys and
loafers who followed at their heels grouped
themselves round to watch. The drummer
quickened his beat and the two banner-bear-
ers stepped forward into the middle of the
little square. They stood there for a moment quite still, the right foot a little in
advance of the other, the left fist on the hip
and the lowered banners drooping from the
right. Then, together, they lifted the
banners and began to wave them round their
heads. In the wind of their motion the flags
opened out. They were the same size and
both of them green and yellow, but the
colours were arranged in a different pattern
on each. And what patterns! Nothing more
"modern" was ever seen. They might have
been designed by Picasso for the Russian
Ballet. Had they been by Picasso, the
graver critics would have called them
futuristic, the sprightlier (I must apologize
for both these expressions) jazz. But the
flags were not Picasso's; they were designed
some four hundred years ago by the name-

less genius who dressed the Sienese for their
yearly pageant. This being the case, the
critics can only take off their hats. The flags
are classical, they are High Art; there is
nothing more to be said.

The drum beat on. The bannermen
waved their flags, so artfully that the whole
expanse of patterned stuff was always un-
furled and tremulously stretched along the
air. They passed the flags from one hand to
the other, behind their backs, under a lifted
leg. Then, at last, drawing themselves together to make a supreme effort, they tossed
their banners into the air. High they rose,
turning slowly, over and over, hung for an
instant at the height of their trajectory, then
dropped back, the weighted stave foremost,
towards their throwers, who caught them as
they fell. A final wave, then the drum returned to its march rhythm, the bannermen
shouldered their flags, and followed by the
anachronistic children and idlers from the
twentieth century, Pinturicchio's three young
bravos swaggered off up the dark street out
of sight and at length, the drum taps coming faintlier and ever faintlier, out of hearing.

Every evening after that, while the swallows were in full cry and flight about the
tower, we heard the beating of the drum.

Every evening, in the little piazza below us,
a fragment of Pinturicchio came to life.
Sometimes it was our friends in green and
yellow who returned to wave their flags
beneath our windows.   Sometimes it was
men from the other *contrade* or districts of
the town, in blue and white, red and white,
black, white and orange, white, green and
red, yellow and scarlet.   Their bright pied
doublets and parti-coloured hose shone out
from among the drabs and funereal blacks
of the twentieth-century crowd that surrounded them.   Their spread flags waved in
the street below, like the painted wings of
enormous butterflies.   The drummer quickened his beat, and to the accompaniment of
a long-drawn rattle, the banners leapt up,
furled and fluttering, into the air.

To the stranger who has never seen a
Palio these little dress rehearsals are richly
promising and exciting.   Charmed by these
present hints, he looks forward eagerly to
what the day itself holds in store.   Even the
Sienese are excited.   The pageant, however
familiar, does not pall on them.   And all the
gambler in them, all the local patriot looks
forward to the result of the race.   Those last
days of June before the first Palio, that
middle week of August before the second,
are days of growing excitement and tension

in Siena.   One enjoys the Palio the more for having lived through them.

Even the mayor and corporation are infected by the pervading excitement.   They are so far carried away that, in the last days of June, they send a small army of men down in the great square before the Palazzo Comunale to eradicate every blade of grass or tuft of moss that can be found growing in the crannies between the flagstones.   It amounts almost to a national characteristic, this hatred of growing things among the works of men.   I have often, in old Italian towns, seen workmen laboriously weeding the less frequented streets and squares.   The Colosseum, mantled till thirty or forty years ago with a romantic, Piranesian growth of shrubs, grasses and flowers, was officially weeded with such extraordinary energy that its ruinousness was sensibly increased.   More stones were brought down in those few months of weeding than had fallen of their own accord in the previous thousand years. But the Italians were pleased; which is, after all, the chief thing that matters.   Their hatred of weeds is fostered by their national pride; a great country, and one which specially piques itself on being modern, cannot allow weeds to grow even among its ruins. I entirely understand and sympathise with

the Italian point of view. If Mr. Ruskin
and his disciples had talked about my house
and me as they talked about Italy and the
Italians, I too should pique myself on being
up-to-date; I should put in bathrooms, central heating and a lift, I should have all the
moss scratched off the walls, I should lay
cork lino on the marble floors. Indeed, I
think that I should probably, in my irrita-
tion, pull down the whole house and build
a new one. Considering the provocation
they have received, it seems to me that the
Italians have been remarkably moderate in
the matter of weeding, destroying and re-
building. Their moderation is due in part,
no doubt, to their comparative poverty.
Their ancestors built with such prodigious
solidity that it would cost as much to pull
down one of their old houses as to build a
new one. Imagine, for example, demolish-
ing the Palazzo Strozzi in Florence. It
would be about as easy to demolish the
Matterhorn. In Rome, which is predomi-
nantly a baroque, seventeenth-century city,
the houses are made of flimsier stuff. Consequently, modernisation progresses there
much more rapidly than in most other Italian
towns. In wealthier England very little antiquity has been permitted to stand. Thus,
most of the great country houses of England

were rebuilt during the eighteenth century.
If Italy had preserved her independence
and her prosperity during the seventeenth,
eighteenth and nineteenth centuries, there
would probably be very much less mediæval
or Renaissance work now surviving than is
actually the case. Money is lacking to mod-
ernize completely. Weeding has the merit
of being cheap and, at the same time, richly
symbolic. When you say of a town that
the grass grows in its streets, you mean that
it is utterly dead. Conversely, if there is no
grass in its streets, it must be alive. No
doubt the mayor and corporation of Siena
did not put the argument quite so explicitly.
But that the argument was put somehow, ob-
scurely and below the surface of the mind,
I do not doubt. The weeding was symbolic
of modernity.

With the weeders came other workmen
who built up round the curving flanks of the
great piazza a series of wooden stands, six
tiers high, for the spectators. The piazza
which is shaped, whether by accident or design I do not know, like an ancient theatre,
became for the time being indeed a theatre.
Between the seats and the central area of the
place, a track was railed off and the slippery
flags covered parsimoniously with sand. Ex-
pectation rose higher than ever.

And at last the day came. The swallows
and swifts wove their arabesques as usual
in the bright golden light above the town.
But their shrill crying was utterly inaudible,
through the deep, continuous, formless mur-
mur of the crowd that thronged the streets
and the great piazza. Under its canopy of
stone the great bell of the Mangia tower
swung incessantly backwards and forwards;
it too seemed dumb. The talking, the laughter, the shouting of forty thousand people
rose up from the piazza in a column of solid
sound, impenetrable to any ordinary noise.

It was after six. We took our places in
one of the stands opposite the Palazzo
Comunale. Our side of the piazza was
already in the shade; but the sun still shone
on the palace and its tall slender tower, making their rosy brickwork glow as though by
inward fire. An immense concourse of
people filled the square and all the tiers
of seats round it. There were people in
every window, even on the roofs. At the
Derby, on boat-race days, at Wembley I
have seen larger crowds; but never, I think,
so many people confined within so small a
space.

The sound of a gunshot broke through the
noise of voices; and at the signal a company
of mounted carabiniers rode into the piazza,

driving the loungers who still thronged the track before them. They were in full dress uniform, black and red, with silver trimmings; cocked hats on their heads and swords in their hands. On their handsome little horses, they looked like a squadron of smart Napoleonic cavalry. The idlers retreated before them, squeezing their way through every convenient opening in the rails into the central area, which was soon densely packed. The track was cleared at a walk and, cleared, was rounded again at the trot, dashingly, in the best Carle Vernet style. The carabiniers got their applause and retired. The crowd waited expectantly. For a moment there was almost a silence. The bell on the tower ceased to be dumb. Some one in the crowd let loose a couple of balloons. They mounted perpendicularly into the still air, a red sphere and a purple. They passed out of the shadow into the sunlight; and the red became a ruby, the purple a glowing amethyst. When they had risen above the level of the roofs, a little breeze caught them and carried them away, still mounting all the time, over our heads, out of sight.

There was another gunshot and Vernet was exchanged for Pinturicchio. The noise of the crowd grew louder as they appeared, the

bell swung, but gave no sound, and across
the square the trumpets of the procession
were all but inaudible. Slowly they marched
round, the representatives of all the seventeen *contrade* of the city. Besides its drummer and its two bannermen, each *contrada*
had a man-at-arms on horseback, three or
four halbardiers and young pages and, if it
happened to be one of the ten competing in
the race, a jockey, all of them wearing the
Pinturicchian livery in its own particular
colours. Their progress was slow; for at
every fifty paces they stopped, to allow the
bannermen to give an exhibition of their skill
with the flags. They must have taken the
best part of an hour to get round. But the
time seemed only too short. The Palio is a
spectacle of which one does not grow tired.
I have seen it three times now and was as
much delighted on the last occasion as on
the first.

English tourists are often sceptical about
the Palio. They remember those terrible
"pageants" which were all the rage some fifteen years ago in their own country, and they
imagine that the Palio will turn out to be
something of the same sort. But let me reassure them; it is not. There is no poetry
by Louis Napoleon Parker at Siena. There
are no choruses of young ladies voicing high

moral sentiments in low voices. There are
no flabby actor-managers imperfectly dis-
guised as Hengist and Horsa, no crowd of
gesticulating supernumeraries dressed in the
worst of taste and the cheapest of bunting.
Nor finally does one often meet at Siena with
that almost invariable accompaniment of the
English pageant—rain. No, the Palio is
just a show; having no "meaning" in particular, but by the mere fact of being traditional and still alive, signifying infinitely
more than the dead-born English affairs for
all their Parkerian blank verse and their
dramatic re-evocations. For these pages and
men-at-arms and bannermen come straight
out of the Pinturicchian past. Their clothes
are those designed for their ancestors, copied
faithfully, once in a generation, in the same
colours and the same rich materials. They
walk, not in cotton or flannelette, but in silks
and furs and velvets. And the colours were
matched, the clothes originally cut by men
whose taste was the faultless taste of the
early Renaissance. To be sure there are cos-
tumiers with as good a taste in these days.
But it was not Paquin, not Lanvin or Poiret
who dressed the actors of the English
pageants; it was professional wig-makers and
lady amateurs. I have already spoken of the
beauty of the flags—the bold, fantastic,

"modern" design of them.   Everything else
at the Palio is in keeping with the flags,
daring, brilliant and yet always right, always
irreproachably refined.   The one false note
is always the *Palio* itself—the painted banner which is given to the *contrada* whose
horse wins the race.   This banner is specially
painted every year for the occasion.   Look at
it, where it comes along, proudly exposed on
the great mediæval war chariot which closes
the procession—look at it, or preferably
don't look at it.   It is a typical property
from the wardrobe of an English pageant
committee.   It is a lady amateur's master-
piece.   Shuddering, one averts the eyes.

Preceded by a line of *quattrocento* pages
carrying festoons of laurel leaves and es-
corted by a company of mounted knights, the
war chariot rolled slowly and ponderously
past, bearing aloft the unworthy trophy.
And by now the trumpets at the head of
the procession sounded, almost inaudibly for
us, from the further side of the piazza.   And
at last the whole procession had made its
round and was lined up in close order in
front of the Palazzo Comunale.   Over the
heads of the spectators standing in the central area, we could see all the thirty-four
banners waving and waving in a last con-
certed display and at last, together, all leap-

ing high into the air, hesitating at the top
of their leap, falling back, out of sight.
There was a burst of applause. The pageant
was over. Another gunshot. And in the
midst of more applause, the racehorses were
ridden to the starting place.

The course is three times round the piazza,
whose shape, as I have said, is something like
that of an ancient theatre. Consequently,
there are two sharp turns, where the ends of
the semicircle meet the straight diameter.
One of these, owing to the irregularity of
the plan, is sharper than the other. The outside wall of the track is padded with mat-
tresses at this point, to prevent impetuous
jockeys who take the corner too fast from
dashing themselves to pieces. The jockeys
ride bareback; the horses run on a thin layer
of sand spread over the flagstones of the
piazza. The Palio is probably the most dangerous flat-race in the world. And it is made
the more dangerous by the excessive patriotism of the rival *contrade*. For the winner
of the race as he reins in his horse after passing the post, is set upon by the supporters
of the other *contrade* (who all think that
their horse should have won), with so real
and earnest a fury that the carabiniers must
always intervene to protect man and beast
from lynching. Our places were at a point

some two or three hundred yards beyond the post, so that we had an excellent view of the battle waged round the winning horse, as he slackened speed.   Scarcely was the post passed when the crowd broke its ranks and rushed out into the course.   Still cantering, the horse came up the track.   A gang of young men ran in pursuit, waving sticks and shouting.   And with them, their Napoleonic coat tails streaming in the wind of their own speed, their cocked hats bobbing, and brandishing their swords in their white-gloved hands, ran the rescuing carabiniers.   There was a brief struggle round the now stationary horse, the young men were repulsed, and surrounded by cocked hats, followed by a crowd of supporters from its native *contrada*, the beast was led off in triumph.   We climbed down from our places.   The piazza was now entirely shaded.   It was only on the upper part of the tower and the battlements of the great Palazzo that the sun still shone. Rosily against the pale blue sky, they glowed. The swifts still turned and turned overhead in the light.   It is said that at evening and at dawn these light-loving birds mount on their strong wings into the sky to bid a last farewell or earliest good-morrow to the sinking or the rising sun.   While we lie sleeping or have resigned ourselves to darkness the swifts are looking down from their watch-tower in the height of heaven over the edge of the turning planet towards the light. Was it a fable, I wondered, looking up at the wheeling birds? Or was it true? Meanwhile, some one was swearing at me for not looking where I was going. I postponed the speculation.

I HAVE always been rather partial to plane geometry; probably because it was the only branch of mathematics that was ever taught me in such a way that I could understand it. For though I have no belief in the power of education to turn public school boys into Newtons (it being quite obvious that, whatever opportunity may be offered, it is only those rare beings desirous of learning and possessing a certain amount of native ability who ever do learn anything), yet I must insist, in my own defence, that the system of mathematical instruction of which, at Eton, I was the unfortunate victim, was calculated not merely to turn my desire to learn into stubborn passive resistance, but also to stifle whatever rudimentary aptitude in this direction I might have possessed. But let that pass. Suffice to say that, in spite of my education and my congenital ineptitude, plane geometry has always charmed me by its simplicity and elegance, its elimination of detail and the individual case, its insistence on generalities.

My love for plane geometry prepared me

to feel a special affection for Holland. For the Dutch landscape has all the qualities that make geometry so delightful. A tour in Holland is a tour through the first books of Euclid. Over a country that is the ideal plane surface of the geometry books, the roads and the canals trace out the shortest distances between point and point. In the interminable polders, the road-topped dykes and gleaming ditches intersect one another at right angles, a criss-cross of perfect parallels. Each rectangle of juicy meadowland contained between the intersecting dykes has identically the same area. Five kilometres long, three deep—the figures record themselves on the clock face of the cyclometre. Five by three by—how many? The demon of calculation possesses the mind. Rolling along those smooth brick roads between the canals, one strains one's eyes to count the dykes at right angles and parallel to one's own. One calculates the area of the polders they enclose. So many square kilometres. But the square kilometres have to be turned into acres. It is a fearful sum to do in one's head; the more so as one has forgotten how many square yards there are in an acre.

And all the time, as one advances the huge geometrical landscape spreads out on either side of the car like an opening fan. Along the level sky-line a score of windmills wave their arms like dancers in a geometrical ballet. Ineluctably, the laws of perspective lead away the long roads and shining waters to a misty vanishing point. Here and there —mere real irrelevancies in the midst of this ideal plain—a few black and white cows out of a picture by Cuyp browse indefatigably in the lush green grass or, remembering Paul Potter, mirror themselves like so many ruminating Narcissi, in the waters of a canal. Sometimes one passes a few human beings, deplorably out of place, but doing their best, generally, to make up for their ungeometrical appearance by mounting bicycles. The circular wheels suggest a variety of new theorems and a new task for the demon of calculation. Suppose the radius of the wheels to be fifteen inches; then fifteen times fifteen times *pi* will be the area. The only trouble is that one has forgotten the value of *pi*.

Hastily I exorcise the demon of calculation that I may be free to admire the farmhouse on the opposite bank of the canal on our right. How perfectly it fits into the geometrical scheme! On a cube, cut down to about a third of its height, is placed a tall pyramid. That is the house. A plantation of trees, set in quincunx formation, surrounds it; the limits of its rectangular garden are drawn in water on the green plain, and beyond these neat ditches extend the interminable flat fields. There are no outhouses, no barns, no farm-yard with untidy stacks. The hay is stored under the huge pyramidal roof, and in the truncated cube below live, on one side the farmer and his family, on the other side (during winter only; for during the rest of the year they sleep in the fields) his black and white Cuyp cows. Every farm-house in North Holland conforms to this type, which is traditional, and so perfectly fitted to the landscape that it would have been impossible to devise anything more suitable. An English farm with its ranges of straggling buildings, its untidy yard, full of animals, its haystacks and pigeon-cotes would be horribly out of place here. In the English landscape, which is all accidents, variety, detail and particular cases, it is perfect. But here, in this generalised and Euclidean North Holland, it would be a blot and a discord. Geometry calls for geometry; with a sense of the æsthetic proprieties which one cannot too highly admire, the Dutch have responded to the appeal of the landscape and have dotted the plane surface of their country with cubes and pyramids.

Delightful landscape! I know of no country that it is more mentally exhilarating to

travel in.   No wonder Descartes preferred
the Dutch to any other scene.   It is the ra-
tionalist's paradise.   One feels as one flies
along in the teeth of one's own forty-mile-
an-hour wind like a Cartesian Encyclopædist
—flushed with mental intoxication, convinced that Euclid is absolute reality, that
God is a mathematician, that the universe is
a simple affair that can be explained in terms
of physics and mechanics, that all men are
equally endowed with reason and that it is
only a question of putting the right arguments before them to make them see the
error of their ways and to inaugurate the
reign of justice and common sense.   Those
were noble and touching dreams, commend-
able inebriations! We are soberer now. We
have learnt that nothing is simple and rational except what we ourselves have invented; that God thinks neither in terms of
Euclid nor of Riemann; that science has "explained" nothing; that the more we know the
more fantastic the world becomes and the
profounder the surrounding darkness; that
reason is unequally distributed; that instinct
is the sole source of action; that prejudice is
incomparably stronger than argument and
that even in the twentieth century men be-
have as they did in the caves of Altamira
and in the lake dwellings of Glastonbury.

And symbolically one makes the same discoveries in Holland. For the polders are not unending, nor all the canals straight, nor every house a wedded cube and pyramid, nor even the fundamental plane surface invariably plane. That delightful "Last Ride Together" feeling that fills one, as one rolls along the brick-topped dykes between the canals, is deceptive. The present is not eternal; the "Last Ride" through plane geometry comes to a sudden end—in a town, in forests, in the sea coast, in a winding river or great estuary. It matters little which; all are fundamentally ungeometrical; each has power to dissipate in an instant all those "paralogisms of rationalism" (as Professor Rougier calls them) which we have so fondly cherished among the polders. The towns have crooked streets thronged with people; the houses are of all shapes and sizes. The coast-line is not straight nor regularly curved and its dunes or its dykes (for it must be defended against the besieging waves by art if not by nature) rear themselves inexcusably out of the plane surface. The woods are unscientific in their shady mysteriousness and one cannot see them for all their individual trees. The rivers are tortuous and alive with boats and barges. The inlets of the sea are entirely shapeless. It is the real world again after the ideal—hopelessly diversified, complex and obscure; but, when the first regrets are over, equally charming with the geometrical landscape we have left behind. We shall find it more charming, indeed, if our minds are practical and extroverted. Personally, I balance my affections. For I love the inner world as much as the outer. When the outer vexes me, I retire to the rational simplicities of the inner—to the polders of the spirit. And when, in their turn, the polders seem unduly flat, the roads too straight and the laws of perspective too tyrannous, I emerge again into the pleasing confusion of untempered reality.

And how beautiful, how curious in Holland that confusion is! I think of Rotterdam with its enormous river and its great bridges, so crowded with the traffic of a metropolis that one has to wait in files, half a mile long, for one's turn to cross. I think of The Hague and how it tries to be elegant and only succeeds in being respectable and upper middle class; of Delft, the commercial city of three hundred years ago; of Haarlem where, in autumn, you see them carting bulbs as in other countries they cart potatoes; of Hoorn on the Zuyder Zee, with its little harbour and seaward-looking castle, its absurd museum filled with rich mixed rubbish, its huge storehouse of cheeses, like an old-fashioned arsenal, where the workmen are busy all day long polishing the yellow cannon balls on a kind of lathe and painting them bright pink with an aniline stain. I think of Volendam—one line of wooden houses perched on the sea wall, and another line crouching in the low green fields behind the dyke. The people at Volendam are dressed as for a musical comedy—*Miss Hook of Holland*—the men in baggy trousers and short jackets, the women in winged white caps, tight bodices, and fifteen superimposed petticoats. Five thousand tourists come daily to look at them; but they still, by some miracle, retain their independence and self-respect. I think of Amsterdam; the old town, like a livelier Bruges, mirrors its high brick houses in the canals. In one quarter an enormous courtesan sits smiling at every window, the meatiest specimens of humanity I ever saw. At nine in the morning, at lunch-time, at six in the afternoon, the streets are suddenly filled with three hundred thousand bicycles; every one, in Amsterdam, goes to and from his business on a pair of wheels. For the pedestrian as well as for the motor-ist it is a nightmare. And they are all trick cyclists. Children of four carry children of three on their handle-bars. Mothers pedal

gaily along with month-old infants sleeping
in cradles fastened to the back carrier. Messenger boys think nothing of taking two
cubic metres of parcels. Dairymen do their
rounds on bicycles specially constructed to
accommodate two hundred quart bottles of
milk in a tray between the two wheels. I
have seen nursery gardeners carrying four
palms and a dozen of potted chrysanthe-
mums on their handle-bars. I have seen five
people riding through the traffic on one machine. The most daring feats of the circus
and the music hall are part of the quotidian
routine in Amsterdam.

I think of the dunes near Schoorl. Seen
from a little distance across the plain they
look like a range of enormous mountains
against the sky. Following with the eye
that jagged silhouette one can feel all the
emotions aroused, shall we say, by the spectacle of the Alps seen from Turin. The
dunes are grand; one could write a canto
from *Childe Harold* about them. And then,
unfortunately, one realises what for a moment one had forgotten, that this line of
formidable peaks is not looking down at one
from fifty miles away, over the curving flank
of the planet; it is just a furlong distant,
and the chimneys of the houses at its base
reach nearly two-thirds of the way to the

top. But what does that matter? With a little good will, I insist, one can feel in Holland all the emotions appropriate to Switzerland.

Yes, they are grand, the dunes of Schoorl and Groet. But I think the grandest sight I saw in non-geometrical Holland was Zaandam—Zaandam from a distance, across the plain.

We had been driving through the polders and the open country of North Holland. Zaandam was the first piece of ungeometrical reality since Alkmaer. Technically, Zaandam is not picturesque; the guide-book has little to say about it. It is a port and manufacturing town on the Zaan, a few miles north of Amsterdam; that is all. They make cocoa there and soap. The air at Zaandam is charged in alternative strata with delicious vapours of molten chocolate and the stench of boiling fat. In wharves by the shores of the river they store American grain and timber from the Baltic. It was the granaries that first announced, from a distance, the presence of Zaandam. Like the cathedrals of a new religion, yet unpreached, they towered up into the hazy autumn air— huge oblongs of concrete set on end, almost windowless, smooth and blankly grey. It was as though their whole force were di-

rected vertically upwards; to look from
windows horizontally across the world would
have been a distraction; eyes were sacrificed
to this upward purpose. And the direction
of that purpose was emphasized by the lines
of the alternately raised and lowered panels
into which the wall spaces of the great buildings were divided—long fine lines of shadow
running up unbrokenly through a hundred
feet from base to summit. The builders of
the papal palace at Avignon used a very
similar device to give their castle its appearance of enormous height and formidable independence. The raised panels and the
shallow blind arches, impossibly long in the
leg, with which they variegated the surface
of the walls, impart to the whole building
an impetuous upward tendency. It is the
same with the grain elevators at Zaandam.
In the haze of autumnal Holland I remembered Provence. And I remembered, as I
watched those towering shapes growing
larger and larger as we approached, Chartres
and Bourges and Reims: gigantic silhouettes
seen at the end of a day's driving, towards
evening, against a pale sky, with the little
lights of a city about their base.

But if at a distance, Zaandam, by its
commercial monuments, reminds one of
Provençal castles and the Gothic cathedrals

of France, a nearer view proclaims it to be unequivocally Dutch. At the foot of the elevators and the only less enormous factories, in the atmosphere of chocolate and soap, lies the straggling town. The suburbs are long, but narrow; for they cling precariously to a knife-edge of land between two waters. The houses are small, made of wood and gaudily painted; with gardens as large as table-cloths, beautifully kept and filled—at any rate at the season when I saw them—with plushy begonias. In one, as large, in this case, as two table-cloths, were no less than fourteen large groups of statuary. In the streets are men in wooden shoes, smoking. Dogs drawing carts with brass pots in them. Innumerable bicycles. It is the real and not the ideal geometrical Holland, crowded, confusing, various, odd, charming. . . . But I sighed as we entered the town. The "Last Ride Together" was over; the dear paralogisms of rationalism were left behind. It was now necessary to face the actual world of men—and to face it, in my case, with precisely five words of Dutch (and patois at that) learned years before for the benefit of a Flemish servant. "Have you fed the cat?" No wonder I regretted the polders.

SABBIONETA

"THEY call it the Palazzo del Te," said
the maid at the little inn in the back
street where we had lunch, "because the Gonzaga used to go and take tea there." And
that was all that she, and probably most
of the other inhabitants of Mantua, knew
about the Gonzaga or their palaces. It
was surprising, perhaps, that she should
have known so much. Gonzaga—the name,
at least, still faintly reverberated. After
two hundred years, how many names are still
remembered? Few indeed. The Gonzaga,
it seems to me, enjoy a degree of immortality
that might be envied them. They have vanished, they are as wholly extinct as the
dinosaur; but in the cities they once ruled
their name still vaguely echoes, and for those
who care to listen they have left behind
some of the most eloquent sermons on the
vanity of human wishes and the mutability
of fortune that stones have ever mutely
preached.

I have seen many ruins and of every
period. Stonehenge and Ansedonia, Ostia
and mediæval Ninfa (which the duke of

Sermoneta is busily turning into the likeness of a neat suburban park), Bolsover and the gruesome modern ruins in northern France. I have seen great cities dead or in decay: Pisa, Bruges and the newly murdered Vienna. But over none, it seemed to me, did there brood so profound a melancholy as over Mantua; none seemed so dead or so utterly bereft of glory; nowhere was desolation more pregnant with the memory of splendour, the silence nowhere so richly musical with echoes. There are a thousand rooms in the labyrinthine Reggia at Mantua —Gothic rooms, rooms of the Renaissance, baroque rooms, rooms rich with the absurd pretentious decorations of the first empire, huge presence chambers and closets and the horribly exquisite apartments of the dwarfs —a thousand rooms, and their walls enclose an emptiness that is the mournful ghost of departed plenitude. It is through Mallarmé's *creux néant musicien* that one walks in Mantua.

And not in Mantua alone. For wherever the Gonzaga lived, they left behind them the same pathetic emptiness, the same pregnant desolation, the same echoes, the same ghosts of splendour.

The Palazzo del Te is made sad and beautiful with the same melancholy as broods in the Reggia. True, the stupid vulgarity of Giulio Romano was permitted to sprawl over its walls in a series of deplorable frescoes (it is curious, by the way, that Giulio Romano should have been the only Italian artist of whom Shakespeare had ever heard, or at least the only one he ever mentioned); but the absurdities and grossnesses seem actually to make the place more touching. The departed tenants of the palace become in a manner more real to one, when one discovers that their taste ran to *trompe l'œil* pictures of fighting giants and mildly pornographic scenes out of pagan mythology. And seeming more human, they seem also more dead; and the void left by their disappearance is more than ever musical with sadness.

Even the cadets of the Gonzaga house enjoyed a power of leaving behind them a more than Pompeian desolation. Twenty miles from Mantua, on the way to Cremona, is a village called Sabbioneta. It lies near the Po, though not on its banks; possesses, for a village, a tolerably large population, mostly engaged in husbandry; is rather dirty and has an appearance—probably quite deceptive—of poverty. In fact it is just like all other villages of the Lombard plain, but with this difference: a Gonzaga once lived here. The squalor of Sabbioneta is no com-

mon squalor; it is a squalor that was once
magnificence. Its farmers and horse-copers
live, dirtily and destructively, in treasures
of late Renaissance architecture. The town
hall is a ducal palace; in the municipal
school, children are taught under carved and
painted ceilings and when the master is out
of the room, they write their names on the
marble bellies of the patient, battered carya-
tids who uphold the scutcheoned mantel.
The weekly cinema show is given in an
Olympic theatre, built a few years after the
famous theatre at Vicenza, by Palladio's
pupil, Scamozzi. The people worship in
sumptuous churches, and if ever soldiers
happen to pass through the town, they are
billeted in the deserted summer palace.

The creator of all these splendours was
Vespasiano, son of that Luigi Gonzaga, the
boon companion of kings, whom, for his
valour and his fabulous strength, his contemporaries nicknamed Rodomonte. Luigi
died young, killed in battle; and his son
Vespasiano was brought up by his aunt,
Giulia Gonzaga, one of the most perfectly
courtly ladies of her age. She had him
taught Latin, Greek, the mathematics, good
manners and the art of war. This last he
practised with distinction, serving at one
time or another under many princes, but

chiefly under Philip II. of Spain, who
honoured him with singular favours. Vespasiano seems to have been the typical
Italian tyrant of his period—cultured, intelligent and only just so much of an un-
governably ferocious ruffian as one would
expect a man to be who has been brought up
in the possession of absolute power. It was
in the intimacy of private life that he displayed his least amiable characteristics. He
poisoned his first wife on a suspicion, probably unfounded, of her infidelity, murdered
her supposed lover and exiled his relations.
His second wife left him mysteriously after
three years of married life and died of pure
misery in a convent, carrying with her into
the grave nobody knew what frightful
secret. His third wife, it is true, lived to
a ripe old age; but then Vespasiano himself
died after only a few years of marriage.
His only son, whom he loved with the
anxious passion of the ambitious parvenu
who desires to found a dynasty, one day
annoyed him by not taking off his cap when
he met him in the street. Vespasiano re-
buked him for this lack of respect. The boy
answered back impertinently. Whereupon
Vespasiano gave him such a frightful kick
in the groin that the boy died. Which shows
that, even when chastising one's own chil-

dren, it is advisable to observe the Queens-
berry rules.

It was in 1560 that Vespasiano decided to
convert the miserable village from which he
took his title into a capital worthy of its
ruler. He set to work with energy. In a
few years the village of squalid cottages
clustering round a feudal castle had given
place to a walled town, with broad streets,
two fine squares, a couple of palaces and a
noble Gallery of Antiques. These last Vespasiano had inherited from his father, Rodomonte, who had been at the sack of Rome in
1527 and had shown himself an industrious
and discriminating looter. Sabbioneta was
in its turn looted by the Austrians, who carried off Rodomonte's spoils to Mantua. The
museum remains; but there is nothing in it
but the *creux néant musicien* which the Gonzaga alone, of all the princes in Italy, had
the special art of creating by their departure.

We had come to Sabbioneta from Parma.
In the vast Farnese palace there is no musically echoing void—merely an ordinary, un-
disturbing emptiness. Only in the colossal
Estensian theatre does one recapture anything like the Mantuan melancholy. We
drove through Colorno, where the last of
the Este built a summer palace about as
large as Hampton Court. Over the Po, by

a bridge of boats, through Casalmaggiore and on, tortuously, by little by-roads across the plain. A line of walls presented themselves, a handsome gate. We drove in, and immediately faint ghostly oboes began to play around us; we were in Sabbioneta among the Gonzaga ghosts.

The central piazza of the town is oblong; Vespasiano's palace stands at one of the shorter ends, presenting to the world a modest façade, five windows wide, once rich with decorations, but now bare. It serves at present as town hall. In the waiting-room on the first floor, stand four life-sized equestrian figures, carved in wood and painted, representing four of Vespasiano's ancestors. Once there was a squadron of twelve; but the rest have been broken up and burned. This crime, together with all the other ravages committed by time or vandals in the course of three centuries, was attributed by the mayor, who personally did us the honours of his municipality, to the socialists who had preceded him in office. It is unnecessary to add that he himself was a fascista.

We walked round in the emptiness under the superbly carved and gilded ceilings. The porter sat among decayed frescoes in the Cabinet of Diana. The town council held its meetings in the Ducal Saloon. The

Gallery of the Ancestors housed a clerk and
the municipal archives. The deputy mayor
had his office in the Hall of the Elephants.
The Sala d'Oro had been turned into an infants' class-room. We walked out again into
the sunlight fairly heart-broken.

The Olympic Theatre is a few yards down
the street. Accompanied by the obliging
young porter from the Cabinet of Diana, we
entered. It is a tiny theatre, but complete
and marvellously elegant. From the pit,
five semi-circular steps rise to a pillared
loggia, behind which—having the width of
the whole auditorium—is the ducal box.
The loggia consists of twelve Corinthian
pillars, topped by a cornice. On the cornice,
above each pillar, stand a dozen stucco gods
and goddesses. Noses and fingers, paps and
ears have gone the way of all art; but the
general form of them survives. Their white
silhouettes gesticulate elegantly against the
twilight of the hall.

The stage was once adorned with a fixed
scene in perspective, like that which Palladio
built at Vicenza. The mayor wanted us to
believe that it was his Bolshevik predecessors
who had destroyed it; but as a matter of
fact it was taken down about a century ago.
Gone, too, are the frescoes with which the
walls were once covered. One year of epi-

demic the theatre was used as a fever hos-
pital. When the plague had passed, it was
thought that the frescoes needed disinfect-
ing; they were thickly white-washed. There
is no money to scrape the white-wash off
again.

We followed the young porter out of the
theatre. Another two or three hundred yards
and we were in the Piazza d'Armi. It is an
oblong, grassy space. On the long axis of
the rectangle, near one end there stands,
handsomely pedestalled, a fluted marble
column, topped by a statue of Athena, the
tutelary goddess of Vespasiano's metropolis.
The pedestal, the capital and the statue are
of the late Renaissance. But the column is
antique, and formed a part of Rodomonte's
Roman booty. Rodomonte was evidently
no petty thief. If a thing is worth doing
it is worth doing thoroughly; that, evidently,
was his motto.

One of the long sides of the rectangle is
occupied by the Gallery of Antiques. It is
a superb building, architecturally by far the
finest thing in the town. The lower storey
consists of an open arcade and the walls of
the gallery above are ornamented with blind
arches, having well-proportioned windows at
the centre of each and separated from one
another by Tuscan pilasters. A very bold

projecting cornice, topped by a low roof, finishes the design, which for sober and massive elegance is one of the most remarkable of its kind with which I am acquainted.

The opposite side of the piazza is open, a hedge separating it from the back gardens of the neighbouring houses. It was here, I fancy, that the feudal castle originally stood. It was pulled down, however, during the eighteenth century (busy Bolsheviks!) and its bricks employed, more usefully but less æsthetically, to strengthen the dykes which defend the surrounding plain, none too impregnably, from the waters of the Po.

Its destruction has left Vespasiano's summer palace, or Palace of the Garden, isolated (save where it joins the Gallery of the Antiques), and rather forlorn at the end of the long piazza. It is a long, low building of only two storeys, rather insignificant from outside. It is evident that Vespasiano built it as economically as he could. For him the place was only a week-end cottage, a holiday resort, whither he could escape from the metropolitan splendour and bustle of the palace in the market-place, a quarter of a mile away. Like all other rulers of small states, Vespasiano must have found it extremely difficult to take an effective holiday. He could not go ten miles in any

direction without coming to a frontier.
Within his dominions it was impossible to
have a change of air. Wisely, therefore,
he decided to concentrate his magnificences.
He built his Balmoral within five minutes'
walk of his Buckingham Palace.

We knocked at the door. The caretaker
who opened to us was an old woman who
might have gone on to any stage and acted
Juliet's Nurse without a moment's rehearsal.
Within the first two minutes of our acquaintance with her she confided to us that she had
just got married—for the third time, at the
age of seventy. Her comments on the con-
nubial state were so very Juliet's Nurse, so
positively Wife-of-Bath, that we were made
to feel quite early-Victorian in comparison
with this robustious old gammer from the
quattrocento. After having told us all that
can be told (and much that cannot be told,
at any rate in polite society) about the married state, she proceeded to do us the honours
of the house. She led the way, opening the
shutters of each room in the long suite, as
we entered it. And as the light came in
through the unglazed windows what Gon-
zagesque ravishments were revealed to us!
There was a Cabinet of Venus, with the
remains of voluptuous nudes, a Hall of the
Winds with puffing cherubs and a mantel in

red marble; a Cabinet of the Cæsars, floored
with marble and adorned with medallions of
all the ruffians of antiquity; a Hall of the
Myths on whose ceiling, vaulted into the
likeness of a truncated pyramid seen from
within, were five delightful scenes from
Lemprière—an Icarus, an Apollo and
Marsyas, a Phaëton, an Arachne and, in
the midst, a to me somewhat mysterious
scene: a naked beauty sitting on the back,
not of a bull (that would have been simple
enough), but of a reclining horse, which
turns its head amorously towards her, while
she caresses its neck. Who was the lady and
who the travestied god I do not rightly know.
Vague memories of an escapade of Saturn's
float through my mind. But perhaps I am
slandering a respectable deity.

But in any case, whatever its subject, the
picture is charming. Vespasiano's principal
artist was Bernardino Campi of Cremona.
He was not a good painter, of course; but at
least he was gracefully and charmingly, instead of vulgarly mediocre, like Giulio
Romano. About the Palazzo del Te there
hangs a certain faded frightfulness; but the
Giardino is all sweetness—mannered, no
doubt, and rather feeble—but none the less
authentic in its ruinous decay.

The old caretaker expounded the pictures

to us as we went round—not out of any
knowledge of what they represented, but
purely out of her imagination, which was a
good deal more interesting.   In the Hall of
the Graces, where the walls are adorned
with what remains of a series of very pretty
little *grotteschi* in the Pompeian manner, her
fancy surpassed itself.   These, she said, were
the records of the Duke's dreams.   Each
time he dreamed a dream he sent for his
painter and had it drawn on the walls of
this room.   These—she pointed to a pair of
Chimæras—he saw in a nightmare; these
dancing satyrs visited his sleep after a merry
evening; these four urns were dreamt of
after too much wine.   As for the three naked
Graces, from whom the room takes its name,
as for those—over the Graces she once more
became too Wife-of-Bath to be recorded.

Her old cracked laughter went echoing
down the empty rooms; and it seemed to
precipitate and crystallize all the melancholy suspended, as it were, in solution
within those bleared and peeling walls.   The
sense of desolation, vaguely felt before, became poignant.   And when the old woman
ushered us into another room, dark and
smelling of mould like the rest, and threw
open the shutters, and called what the light
revealed the "Hall of the Mirrors," I could

almost have wept. For in the Hall of the
Mirrors there are no more mirrors, only the
elaborate framing of them on walls and ceiling. Where the glasses of Murano once
shone are spaces of bare plaster that stare
out like blind eyes, blankly and, it seems
after a little, reproachfully. "They used to
dance in this room," said the old woman.

Part III: Works of Art

MOST of our mistakes are fundamentally grammatical. We create our own difficulties by employing an inadequate language to describe facts. Thus, to take one example, we are constantly giving the same name to more than one thing, and more than one name to the same thing. The results, when we come to argue, are deplorable. For we are using a language which does not adequately describe the things about which we are arguing.

The word "painter" is one of those names whose indiscriminate application has led to the worst results. All those who, for whatever reason and with whatever intentions, put brushes to canvas and make pictures, are called without distinction, painters. Deceived by the uniqueness of the name æstheticians have tried to make us believe that there is a single painter-psychology, a single function of painting, a single standard of criticism. Fashion changes and the views of art critics with it. At the present time it is fashionable to believe in form to the exclusion of subject. Young people almost swoon away with excess of æsthetic emotion before a Matisse. Two generations ago they would have been wiping their eyes before the latest Landseer. (Ah, those more than human, those positively Christ-like dogs—how they moved, what lessons they taught! There had been no religious painting like Landseer's since Carlo Dolci died.)

These historical considerations should make us chary of believing too exclusively in any single theory of art. One kind of painting, one set of ideas are fashionable at any given moment. They are made the basis of a theory which condemns all other kinds of painting and all preceding critical theories. The process constantly repeats itself.

At the present moment, it is true, we have achieved an unprecedentedly tolerant eclecticism. We are able, if we are up-to-date to enjoy everything, from negro sculpture to Lucca della Robbia and from Magnasco to Byzantine mosaics. But it is an eclecticism achieved at the expense of almost the whole content of the various works of art considered. What we have learned to see in all these works is their formal qualities, which we abstract and arbitrarily call essential. The subject of the work, with all that the painter desired to express in it beyond his feelings about formal relations, contemporary criticism rejects as unimportant. The young painter scrupulously avoids introducing into his pictures anything that might be mistaken for a story, or the expression of a view of life, while the young *Kunstforscher* turns, as though at an act of exhibitionism, from any manifestation by a contemporary of any such forbidden interest in drama or philosophy. True, the old masters are indulgently permitted to illustrate stories and express their thoughts about the world. Poor devils, they knew no better! Your modern observer makes allowance for their ignorance and passes over in silence all that is not a matter of formal relations. The admirers of Giotto (as numerous to-day as were the admirers of Guido Reni a hundred years ago) contrive to look at the master's frescoes without considering what they represent, or what the painter desired to express. Every germ of drama or meaning is disinfected out of them; only the composition is admired. The process is analogous to reading Latin verses without understanding them—simply for the sake of the rhythmical rumbling of the hexameters.

It would be absurd, of course, to deny the importance of formal relations. No picture can hold together without composition and

no good painter is without some specific passion for form as such—just as no good writer
is without a passion for words and the arrangement of words.   It is obvious that no
man can adequately express himself, unless
he takes an interest in the terms which he
proposes to use as his medium of expression.
Not all painters are interested in the same
sort of forms.   Some, for example, have a
passion for masses and the surfaces of solids.
Others delight in line.   Some compose in
three dimensions.   Others like to make silhouettes on the flat.   Some like to make
the surface of the paint smooth and, as it
were, translucent, so that the objects represented in the picture can be seen distinct and
separate, as through a sheet of glass.   Others
(as for example Rembrandt) love to make
a rich thick surface which shall absorb and
draw together into one whole all the objects
represented, and that in spite of the depth
of the composition and the distance of the
objects from the plane of the picture.   All
these purely æsthetic considerations are, as I
have said, important.   All artists are interested in them; but almost none are interested
in them to the exclusion of everything else.
It is very seldom indeed that we find a
painter who can be inspired merely by his
interest in form and texture to paint a pic-

ture. Good painters of "abstract" subjects
or even of still lives are rare. Apples and
solid geometry do not stimulate a man to
express his feelings about form and make a
composition. All thoughts and emotions are
interdependent. In the words of the dear
old song,

> The roses round the door
> Make me love mother more.

One feeling is excited by another. Our
faculties work best in a congenial emotional
atmosphere. For example, Mantegna's
faculty for making noble arrangements of
forms was stimulated by his feelings about
heroic and god-like humanity. Expressing
those feelings, which he found exciting, he
also expressed—and in the most perfect
manner of which he was capable—his feelings about masses, surfaces, solids, and
voids. "The roses round the door"—his
hero worship—"made him love mother
more"—made him, by stimulating his faculty for composition, paint better. If Isa-
bella d'Este had made him paint apples,
table napkins and bottles, he would have
produced, being uninterested in these objects,
a poor composition. And yet, from a purely
formal point of view, apples, bottles and

napkins are quite as interesting as human bodies and faces. But Mantegna—and with him the majority of painters—did not happen to be very passionately interested in these inanimate objects. When one is bored one becomes boring.

> The apples round the door
> Make me a frightful bore.

Inevitably; unless I happen to be so exclusively interested in form that I can paint anything that has a shape; or unless I happen to possess some measure of that queer pantheism, that animistic superstition which made Van Gogh regard the humblest of common objects as being divinely or devilishly alive. *"Crains dans le mur aveugle un regard qui t'épie."* If a painter can do that, he will be able, like Van Gogh, to make pictures of cabbage fields and the bedrooms of cheap hotels that shall be as wildly dramatic as a Rape of the Sabines.

The contemporary fashion is to admire beyond all others the painter who can concentrate on the formal side of his art and produce pictures which are entirely devoid of literature. Old Renoir's apophthegm, *"Un peintre, voyez-vous, qui a le sentiment du téton et des fesses, est un homme sauvé,"* is

considered by the purists suspiciously lati-
tudinarian. A painter who has the sentiment
of the pap and the buttocks is a painter who
portrays real models with gusto. Your pure
æsthete should only have a feeling for hemi-
spheres, curved lines and surfaces. But this
"sentiment of the buttocks" is common to
all good painters. It is the lowest common
measure of the whole profession. It is possible, like Mantegna, to have a passionate
feeling for all that is solid, and at the same
time to be a stoic philosopher and a hero-
worshipper; possible, with Michelangelo, to
have a complete realization of breasts and
also an interest in the soul or, like Rubens,
to have a sentiment for human greatness as
well as for human rumps. The greater in-
cludes the less; great dramatic or reflective
painters know everything that the æstheticians who paint geometrical pictures, apples
or buttocks know, and a great deal more besides. What they have to say about formal
relations, though important, is only a part
of what they have to express. The contemporary insistence on form to the exclusion of
everything else is an absurdity. So was the
older insistence on exact imitation and sentiment to the exclusion of form. There need
be no exclusions. In spite of the single
name, there are many different kinds of

painters and all of them, with the exception of those who cannot paint, and those whose minds are trivial, vulgar and tedious, have a right to exist.

All classifications and theories are made after the event; the facts must first occur before they can be tabulated and methodized. Reversing the historical process, we attack the facts forearmed with theoretical prejudice. Instead of considering each fact on its own merits, we ask how it fits into the theoretical scheme. At any given moment a number of meritorious facts fail to fit into the fashionable theory and have to be ignored. Thus El Greco's art failed to conform with the ideal of good painting held by Philip the Second and his contemporaries. The Sienese primitives seemed to the seventeenth and eighteenth centuries incompetent barbarians. Under the influence of Ruskin, the later nineteenth century contrived to dislike almost all architecture that was not Gothic. And the early twentieth century, under the influence of the French, deplores and ignores, in painting, all that is literary, reflective or dramatic.

In every age theory has caused men to like much that was bad and reject much that was good. The only prejudice that the ideal art critic should have is against the incompetent, the mentally dishonest and the futile. The number of ways in which good pictures can be painted is quite incalculable, depending only on the variability of the human mind. Every good painter invents a new way of painting. Is this man a competent painter? Has he something to say, is he genuine? These are the questions a critic must ask himself. Not, Does he conform with my theory of imitation, or distortion, or moral purity, or significant form?

There is one painter against whom, it seems to me, theoretical prejudice has always most unfairly told. I mean the elder Breughel. Looking at his best paintings I find that I can honestly answer in the affirmative all the questions which a critic may legitimately put himself. He is highly competent æsthetically; he has plenty to say; his mind is curious, interesting and powerful; and he has no false pretensions, is entirely honest. And yet he has never enjoyed the high reputation to which his merits entitle him. This is due, I think, to the fact that his work has never quite squared with any of the various critical theories which since his days have had a vogue in the æsthetic world.

A subtle colourist, a sure and powerful draughtsman, and possessing powers of composition that enable him to marshal the innumerable figures with which his pictures are filled into pleasingly decorative groups (built up, as we see, when we try to analyse his methods of formal arrangement, out of individually flat, silhouette-like shapes standing in a succession of receding planes) Breughel can boast of purely æsthetic merits that ought to endear him even to the strictest sect of the Pharisees. Coated with this pure æsthetic jam, the bitter pill of his literature might easily, one would suppose, be swallowed. If Giotto's dalliance with sacred history be forgiven him, why may not Breughel be excused for being an anthropologist and a social philosopher? To which I tentatively answer: Giotto is forgiven, because we have so utterly ceased to believe in Catholic Christianity that we can easily ignore the subject matter of his pictures and concentrate only on their formal qualities; Breughel, on the other hand, is unforgivable because he made comments on humanity that are still interesting to us. From his subject matter we cannot escape; it touches us too closely to be ignored. That is why Breughel is despised by all up-to-date *Kunstforschers*.

And even in the past, when there was no theoretical objection to the mingling of literature and painting, Breughel failed, for another reason, to get his due. He was considered low, gross, a mere comedian, and as such unworthy of serious consideration. Thus, the *Encyclopædia Britannica*, which in these matters may be safely relied on to give the current opinion of a couple of generations ago, informs us, in the eleven lines which it parsimoniously devotes to Peter Breughel that "the subjects of his pictures are chiefly humorous figures, like those of D. Teniers; and if he wants the delicate touch and silvery clearness of that master, he has abundant spirit and comic power."

Whoever wrote these words—and they might have been written by any one desirous, fifty years ago, of playing for safety and saying the right thing—can never have taken the trouble to look at any of the pictures by Breughel when he was a grown and accomplished artist.

In his youth, it is true, he did a great deal of hack work for a dealer who specialized in caricatures and devils in the manner of Hieronymus Bosch. But his later pictures, painted when he had really mastered the secrets of his art, are not comic at all. They are studies of peasant life, they are allegories, they are religious pictures of the most strangely reflective cast, they are exquisitely poetical landscapes. Breughel died at the height of his powers. But there is enough of his mature work in existence—at Antwerp, at Brussels, at Naples and above all at Vienna—to expose the fatuity of the classical verdict and exhibit him for what he was: the first landscape painter of his century, the acutest student of manners, and the wonderfully skilful pictorial expounder or suggester of a view of life. It is at Vienna, indeed, that Breughel's art can best be studied in all its aspects. For Vienna possesses practically all his best pictures of whatever kind. The scattered pictures at Antwerp, Brussels, Paris, Naples and elsewhere give one but the faintest notion of Breughel's powers. In the Vienna galleries are collected more than a dozen of his pictures, all belonging to his last and best period. The Tower of Babel, the great Calvary, the Numbering of the People at Bethlehem, the two Winter Landscapes and the Autumn Landscape, the Conversion of Saint Paul, the Battle between the Israelites and the Philistines, the Marriage Feast and the Peasants' Dance—all these admirable works are here. It is on these that he must be judged.

There are four landscapes at Vienna: the Dark Day (January) and Huntsmen in the Snow (February), a November landscape (the Return of the Cattle), and the Numbering of the People at Bethlehem which in spite of its name is little more than a landscape with figures. This last, like the February Landscape and the Massacre of the Innocents at Brussels, is a study of snow. Snow scenes lent themselves particularly well to Breughel's style of painting. For a snowy background has the effect of making all dark or coloured objects seen against it appear in the form of very distinct, sharp-edged silhouettes. Breughel does in all his compositions what the snow does in nature. All the objects in his pictures (which are composed in a manner that reminds one very much of the Japanese) are paper-thin silhouettes arranged, plane after plane, like the theatrical scenery in the depth of the stage. Consequently in the painting of snow scenes, where nature starts by imitating his habitual method, he achieves an almost disquieting degree of fundamental realism. Those hunters stepping down over the brow of the hill towards the snowy valley with its frozen ponds are Jack Frost himself and his crew. The crowds who move about the white streets of Bethlehem have their being in an absolute winter, and those ferocious troopers looting and innocent-hunting in the midst of a Christmas card landscape are a part of the very army of winter, and the innocents they kill are the young green shoots of the earth.

Breughel's method is less fundamentally compatible with the snowless landscapes of January and November. The different planes stand apart a little too flatly and distinctly. It needs a softer, bloomier kind of painting to recapture the intimate quality of such scenes as those he portrays in these two pictures. A born painter of Autumn, for example, would have fused the beasts, the men, the trees and the distant mountains into a hazier unity, melting all together, the near and the far, in the rich surface of his paint. Breughel painted too transparently and too flatly to be the perfect interpreter of such landscapes. Still, even in terms of his not entirely suitable convention he has done marvels. The Autumn Day is a thing of the most exquisite beauty. Here, as in the more sombrely dramatic January Landscape, he makes a subtle use of golds and yellows and browns, creating a sober yet luminous harmony of colours. The November Landscape is entirely placid and serene; but in the Dark Day he has staged one of those natural dramas of the sky and earth—a conflict between light and darkness. Light breaks from under clouds along the horizon, shines up from the river in the valley that lies in the middle distance, glitters on the peaks of the mountains. The foreground, which represents the crest of a wooded hill, is dark; and the leafless trees growing on the slopes are black against the sky. These two pictures are the most beautiful sixteenth-century landscapes of which I have any knowledge. They are intensely poetical, yet sober and not excessively picturesque or romantic. Those fearful crags and beetling precipices of which the older painters were so fond do not appear in these examples of Breughel's maturest work.

Breughel's anthropology is as delightful as his nature poetry. He knew his Flemings, knew them intimately, both in their prosperity and during the miserable years of strife, of rebellion, of persecution, of war and consequent poverty which followed the advent of the Reformation in Flanders.

A Fleming himself, and so profoundly and ineradicably a Fleming that he was able to go to Italy, and, like his great countryman in the previous century, Roger van der Weyden, return without the faintest tincture of Italianism—he was perfectly qualified to be the natural historian of the Flemish folk. He exhibits them mostly in those moments of orgiastic gaiety with which they temper the laborious monotony of their daily lives: eating enormously, drinking, uncouthly dancing, indulging in that peculiarly Flemish scatological waggery. The Wedding Feast and the Peasants' Dance, both at Vienna, are superb examples of this anthropological type of painting. Nor must we forget those two curious pictures, the Battle Between Carnival and Lent and the Children's Games. They too show us certain aspects of the joyous side of Flemish life. But the view is not of an individual scene, casually seized at its height and reproduced. These two pictures are systematic and encyclopædic. In one he illustrates all children's games; in the other all the amusements of carnival, with all the forces arrayed on the side of asceticism. In the same way he represents, in his extraordinary Tower of Babel, all the processes of building. These pictures are handbooks of their respective subjects.

Breughel's fondness for generalizing and systematizing is further illustrated in his allegorical pieces. The Triumph of Death, at the Prado, is appalling in its elaboration and completeness. The fantastic "Dulle Griet" at Antwerp is an almost equally elaborate triumph of evil. His illustrations to proverbs and parables belong to the same class. They show him to have been a man profoundly convinced of the reality of evil and of the horrors which this mortal life, not to mention eternity, hold in store for suffering humanity. The world is a horrible place; but in spite of this, or precisely because of this, men and women eat, drink and dance, Carnival tilts against Lent and triumphs, if only for a moment; children play in the streets, people get married in the midst of gross rejoicings.

But of all Breughel's pictures the one most richly suggestive of reflection is not specifically allegorical or systematic. Christ carrying the Cross is one of his largest canvases, thronged with small figures rhythmically grouped against a wide and romantic background. The composition is simple, pleasing in itself, and seems to spring out of the subject instead of being imposed on it. So much for pure æsthetics.

Of the Crucifixion and the Carrying of the Cross there are hundreds of representations by the most admirable and diverse masters. But of all that I have ever seen this Calvary of Breughel's is the most suggestive and, dramatically, the most appalling. For all other masters have painted these dreadful scenes from within, so to speak, outwards. For them Christ is the

centre, the divine hero of the tragedy; this
is the fact from which they start; it affects
and transforms all the other facts, justify-
ing, in a sense, the horror of the drama and
ranging all that surrounds the central figure
in an ordered hierarchy of good and evil.
Breughel, on the other hand, starts from the
outside and works inwards.   He represents
the scene as it would have appeared to any
casual spectator on the road to Golgotha on
a certain spring morning in the year 33 A.D.
Other artists have pretended to be angels,
painting the scene with a knowledge of its
significance.   But Breughel resolutely remains a human onlooker.   What he shows
is a crowd of people walking briskly in holiday joyfulness up the slopes of a hill.   On
the top of the hill, which is seen in the
middle distance on the right, are two crosses
with thieves fastened to them, and between
them a little hole in the ground in which
another cross is soon to be planted.   Round
the crosses, on the bare hill top stands a
ring of people, who have come out with their
picnic baskets to look on at the free entertainment offered by the ministers of justice.
Those who have already taken their stand
round the crosses are the prudent ones; in
these days we should see them with camp
stools and thermos flasks, six hours ahead

of time, in the vanguard of the queue for a
Melba night at Covent Garden.   The less
provident or more adventurous people are in
the crowd coming up the hill with the third
and greatest of the criminals whose cross is
to take the place of honour between the other
two.   In their anxiety not to miss any of
the fun on the way up, they forget that they
will have to take back seats at the actual
place of execution.   But it may be, of course,
that they have reserved their places, up
there.   At Tyburn one could get an excellent seat in a private box for half a crown;
with the ticket in one's pocket, one could
follow the cart all the way from the prison,
arrive with the criminal and yet have a perfect view of the performance.   In these later
days, when cranky humanitarianism has so
far triumphed that hangings take place in
private and Mrs. Thompson's screams are
not even allowed to be recorded on the radio,
we have to be content with reading about
executions, not with seeing them.   The im-
presarios who sold seats at Tyburn have
been replaced by titled newspaper proprietors who sell juicy descriptions of
Tyburn to a prodigiously much larger
public.   If people were still hanged at
Marble Arch, Lord Riddell would be much
less rich.

That eager, tremulous, lascivious interest in blood and beastliness which in these more civilized days we can only satisfy at one remove from reality in the pages of our newspapers, was franklier indulged in Breughel's day; the naïve ingenuous brute in man was less sophisticated, was given longer rope, and joyously barks and wags its tail round the appointed victim.   Seen thus, impassively, from the outside, the tragedy does not purge or uplift; it appals and makes desperate; or it may even inspire a kind of gruesome mirth. The same situation may often be either tragic or comic, according as it is seen through the eyes of those who suffer or those who look on.   (Shift the point of vision a little and Macbeth could be paraphrased as a roaring farce.)   Breughel makes a concession to the high tragic convention by placing in the foreground of his picture a little group made up of the holy women weeping and wringing their hands.   They stand quite apart from the other figures in the picture and are fundamentally out of harmony with them, being painted in the style of Roger van der Weyden.   A little oasis of passionate spirituality, an island of consciousness and comprehension in the midst of the pervading stupidity and brutishness.   Why Breughel put them into his picture is difficult to guess;

perhaps for the benefit of the conventionally
religious, perhaps out of respect for tradition, perhaps he found his own creation too
depressing and added this noble irrelevance
to reassure himself.

RIMINI AND ALBERTI

RIMINI was honoured, that morning, by the presence of three distinguished visitors—ourselves and the Thaumaturgical Arm of St. Francis Xavier. Divorced from the rest of the saint's remains, whose home is a jewelled tabernacle in the church of Jesus at Old Goa, the Arm, like ourselves, was making an Italian tour. But while we poor common tourists were spending money on the way, the Thaumaturgical Arm—and this was perhaps its most miraculous achievement—was raking it in. It had only to show itself through the crystal window of the reliquary in which it travelled —a skeleton arm, with a huge amethyst ring still glittering on one of the fingers of its bony hand—to command the veneration of all beholders and a copper collection, thinly interspersed with nickel and the smallest paper. The copper collection went to the foreign missions: what happened to the veneration, I do not venture to guess. It was set down, no doubt, with their offered pence, to the credit of those who felt it, in the recording angel's book.

I felt rather sorry for St. Francis Xavier's arm. The body of the saint, after translation from China to Malacca and from Malacca to India, now reposes, as I have said, in the gaudy shrine at Goa. After a life so extraordinarily strenuous as was his, the great missionary deserves to rest in peace. And so he does, most of him. But his right arm has had to forgo its secular quiet; its missionary voyages are not yet over. In its gold and crystal box it travels indefatigably through catholic Christendom collecting pence—"for spoiling Indian innocence," as Mr. Matthew Green tersely and rather tartly put it, two hundred years ago. Poor Arm!

We found it, that morning, in the church of San Francesco at Rimini. A crowd of adorers filled the building and overflowed into the street outside. The people seemed to be waiting rather vaguely in the hope of something thaumaturgical happening. Within the church, a long queue of men and women shuffled slowly up into the choir to kiss the jewelled bone-box and deposit their *soldi*. Outside, among the crowd at the door of the church, stood a number of hawkers, selling picture postcards of the Thaumaturgical Arm and brief but fabulous biographies of its owner. We got into conversation with one of them, who told us that he followed the Arm from town to town, selling his wares wherever it stopped to show itself. The business seemed a tolerably profitable one; it enabled him, at any rate, to keep a wife and family living in comfort at Milan. He showed us their photographs; mother and children—they all looked well nourished. But, poor fellow! his business kept him almost uninterruptedly away from home. "What does one marry for?" he said as he put the photographs back into his pocket. "What?" He sighed and shook his head. If only the Arm could be induced to settle down for a little!

During the lunch hour the Arm was taken for a drive round Rimini. Red and yellow counterpanes were hung out of all the windows in its honour; the faithful waited impatiently. And at last it came, driving in a very large, very noisy and dirty old Fiat, accompanied, not, as one might have expected, by the ecclesiastical dignitaries of the city, but by seven or eight very secular young men in black shirts, with frizzy hair, their trouser pockets bulging with automatic pistols—the committee of the local fascio, no doubt.

The Arm occupied the front seat, next the driver: the fascists lolled behind. As the car passed, the faithful did a very curious thing; mingling the gestures of reverence and applause, they fell on their knees and clapped their hands. The Arm was treated as though it were a combination of Jackie Coogan and the Host. After lunch, it was driven rapidly away to Bologna. The vendors of sacred pictures followed as fast as the Italian train would take them, the crowd dispersed and the church of San Francesco reverted to its habitual silence.

For this we were rather glad; for it was not to see a fragment of St. Francis Xavier that we had come to Rimini; it was to look at the church of St. Francis of Assisi. Sightseeing, so long as the Arm was there, had been impossible; its departure left us free to look round at our ease. Still, I was very glad that we had seen the peripatetic relic and its adorers in San Francesco. In this strange church which Malatesta found a Christian temple, rebuilt in pagan form and rededicated to himself, his mistress and the humanities, the scenes we had just witnessed possessed a certain piercing incongruousness that provoked—the wit of circumstances—a kind of meditative mirth. I tried to imagine what the first St. Francis would have thought of Sigismondo Malatesta, what Sigismondo thought of him and how he would have regarded the desecration of his

Nietzschean temple by this posthumous visit
of a bit of the second St. Francis. One can
imagine a pleasant little Gobinesque or
Lucianic dialogue between the four of them
in the Elysian Fields, a light and airy skat-
ing over the most fearful depths of the spirit.
And for those who have ears to hear there
is eloquence in the dumb disputation of the
stones. The Gothic arches of the interior
protest against the Roman shell with which
Alberti enclosed St. Francis's church; protest
against Matteo de' Pasti's pagan decorations and Malatesta's blasphemous self-
exaltation; protest, while they commend
the missionary's untiring disinterestedness,
against the excessive richness of his Jesuit
reliquary. Grave, restrained, and intellectual, Alberti's classical façade seems to deplore the *naïveté* of the first St. Francis and
the intolerant enthusiasms of the second,
and, praising Malatesta's intelligence, to re-
buke him for his lusts and excesses. Malatesta, meanwhile, laughs cynically at all of
them. Power, pleasure and Isotta—these,
he announces, through the scheme of decorations which he made Matteo de' Pasti
carry out, these are the only things that
matter.

The exterior of the church is entirely
Alberti's. Neither St. Francis nor Mala-

testa are allowed to disturb its solemn and harmonious beauty. Its façade is a triumphal arch, a nobler version of that arch of Augustus which spans the street at the other end of Rimini. In the colossal thickness of the southern wall, Alberti has pierced a series of deep arched niches. Recessed shadow alternates harmoniously down a long perspective with smooth sunlit stone; and in every niche, plain and severe like the character of an early Roman in the pages of Plutarch, stands the sarcophagus of a scholar or a philosopher. There is nothing here of St. Francis's pre-lapsarian ingenuousness. Alberti is an entirely conscious adult; he worships, but worships reason, rationally. The whole building is a hymn to intellectual beauty, an exaltation of reason as the only source of human greatness. Its form is Roman; for Rome was the retrospective Utopia in which such men as Alberti, from the time of the Renaissance down to a much later date, saw the fulfilment of their ideals. The Roman myth dies hard, the Greek harder still; there are certain victims of a classical education who still regard the Republic as the home of all virtues and see in Periclean Athens the unique repository of human intelligence.

Malatesta would have got a better personal apotheosis if he had lived in a later century. Alberti was too severe and stoical an artist to condescend to mere theatrical grandiosity. Nor, indeed, was the art of being grandiose really understood till the seventeenth century, the age of baroque, of kingly and clerical display. The hard-working missionary, whose arm we had seen that morning in Malatesta's temple, reposes at Goa in the sort of surroundings that would be perfectly suitable in a tyrant's self-raised shrine. Alberti's monument, on the contrary, is a tribute to intellectual greatness. As a memorial to a particularly cunning and murderous ruffian it is absurd.

In the interior of the church, it is true, Malatesta had things all his own way. Alberti was not there to interfere in his scheme of decoration, so that Sigismondo was able to dictate to Matteo de' Pasti and his colleagues all the themes of their carving. The interior is consequently one vast personal tribute to Malatesta and Isotta, with an occasional good word in favour of the pagan gods, of literature, art and science. The too expressive theatrical gesture of the baroque architects and decorators had not yet been invented; Sigismondo's vulgar tyranny is consequently celebrated in the most perfect taste and in terms of a delicate and learned fantasy. Sigismondo got better than his deserts; he deserved Borromini, the Cavaliere Arpino and a tenth-rate imitator of Bernini. What he actually got, owing to the accident of his date, was Matteo de' Pasti, Piero della Francesca and Leon Battista Alberti.

Alberti's share in the monument, then, is a kind of hymn to intellectual beauty, a pæan in praise of civilization, couched in the language of Rome—but freely and not pedantically employed, as the philosophers and the poets of the age employed the Latin idiom. To my mind, he was almost the noblest Roman of them all. The exterior of San Francesco at Rimini, the interior of Sant' Andrea at Mantua (sadly daubed about by later decorators and with Juvara's absurd high-drummed cupola in the midst instead of the saucer dome designed by Alberti himself) are as fine as anything in the whole range of Renaissance architecture. What renders them the more remarkable is that they were without precedent, in his age. Alberti was one of the re-inventors of the style. Of this particular Roman manner, indeed (the manner which became the current idiom of the later Renaissance) he was the sole re-discoverer. The other early Renaissance manner, based, like Alberti's, on

the classics—the manner of Brunelleschi—
was doomed, so far at any rate as ecclesiastical architecture was concerned, to extinction.
Sant' Andrea at Mantua is the model from
which the typical churches of the later
Renaissance were imitated, not Brunelleschi's
Florentine San Lorenzo or Santo Spirito.

A comparison between these nearly contemporary architects—Brunelleschi was born
some twenty-five years before Alberti—is extremely interesting and instructive.   Both
were enthusiastic students of the antique,
both knew their Rome, both employed in
their buildings the characteristic elements of
classical architecture.   And yet it would be
difficult to discover two architects whose
work is more completely dissimilar.   Compare the interiors of Brunelleschi's two Florentine churches with that of Alberti's Sant'
Andrea.   Brunelleschi's churches are divided
into a nave and aisles by rows of tall slender
pillars supporting round arches.   The details
are classical and so correct that they might
have been executed by Roman workmen.
But the general design is not Roman, but
Romanesque.   His churches are simply more
spidery versions of eleventh-century basil-
icas, with "purer" details.   All is airiness
and lightness; there is even a certain air of
insecurity about these church interiors, so

slender are the pillars, so much free space is to be seen.

What a contrast with Alberti's great church! It is built in the form of a Latin cross, with a single nave and side chapels. The nave is barrel-vaulted; over the crossing is a dome (Juvara's, unfortunately, not Alberti's); the altar is placed in an apse. The chapels open on to the central nave by tall, and proportionately wide, round-headed arches. Between each of the chapels is a gigantic pier of masonry, as wide as the arches which they separate. A small door is pierced in each of these piers, giving access to subsidiary chapels hollowed out of their mass. But the doors are inconspicuous and the general effect is one of void and solid equally alternating. Alberti's is essentially the architecture of masses, Brunelleschi's of lines. Even to the enormous dome of Santa Maria del Fiore Brunelleschi contrives to impart an extraordinary lightness, as of lines with voids between them. The huge mass hangs aerially from its eight ribs of marble. A miracle is effortlessly consummated before our eyes. But a dome, however light you make it, is essentially an affair of masses. In designing his cupola for Santa Maria del Fiore Brunelleschi found the plastic view of things imposed upon him. That is why, it may be, the dome is so incomparably the finest thing he ever made. He was not permitted by the nature of the architectural problem to be solved to give free play to his passion for lightness and the fine line. He was dealing here with masses; it could not be escaped. The result was that, treating the mass of the dome as far as was possible in terms of light, strong, leaping lines, he contrived to impart to his work an elegance and an aerial strength such as have never been equalled in any other dome. The rest of Brunelleschi's work, however charming and graceful, is, to my mind at any rate, far less satisfying, precisely because it is so definitely an affair of lines. Brunelleschi studied the architecture of the Romans; but he took from it only its details. What was essential in it—its majestic massiveness— did not appeal to him. He preferred, in all his church designs, to refine and refine on the work of the Romanesque architects, until at last he arrived at a slender and precarious elegance that was all vacuum and outline.

Alberti on the other hand, took from the Romans their fundamental conception of an architecture of masses and developed it, with refinements, for modern, Christian uses. To my mind, he was the better and truer architect of the two. For I personally like massiveness and an air of solidity. Others, I know, prefer lines and lightness and would put the interior of San Lorenzo above that of Sant' Andrea, the Pazzi chapel above San Francesco at Rimini. We shall never be reconciled. All who practise the visual arts and, presumably, all who appreciate them must have some kind of feeling for form as such. But not all are interested in the same kind of forms. The lovers of pure line and the lovers of mass stand at opposite ends of an æsthetic scale. The æsthetic passion of one artist, or one art lover, is solidity; another is moved only by linear arabesques on a flat surface. Those formal passions may be misplaced. Painters may be led by their excessive love of three-dimensional solidity quite beyond the field of painting; Michelangelo is an obvious example. Sculptors with too great a fondness for mere linear effect cease to be sculptors, and their work is no more than a flat decoration in stone or metal, meant to be seen from only one point of view and having no depth; the famous Diana attributed to Goujon (but probably by Benvenuto Cellini) is one of these statues conceived in the flat. Just as painters must not be too fond of solidity, nor sculptors too much attached to flatness, so, it seems to me, no architect should be too exclusively interested in lines. Architecture in the hands of a linear enthusiast takes on the too slender, spidery elegance of Brunelleschi's work.

The psycho-analysts, who trace all interest in art back to an infantile love of excrement, would doubtless offer some simple fæcal explanation for the varieties in our æsthetic passions. One man loves masses, another lines: the explanation in terms of coprophily is so obvious that I may be excused from giving it here. I will content myself by quoting from the works of Dr. Ernest Jones, the reason why the worship of form should come to be connected in so many cases with the worship of a moral ideal; in a word why art is so often religious. "Religion," says Dr. Jones, "has always used art in one form or another, and must do so, for the reason that incestuous desires invariably construct their phantasies out of the material provided by the unconscious memory of infantile coprophilic interests; that is the inner meaning of the phrase, 'Art is the handmaid of Religion.'" Illuminating and beautiful words! It is a pity they were not written thirty years ago. I should have liked to read Tolstoi's comments in *What is Art?* on this last and best of the æsthetic theories.

CONXOLUS

TO know what everybody else knows—
that Virgil, for example, wrote the
Æneid, or that the sum of the angles of a
triangle is equal to two right angles—is
rather boring and undistinguished. If you
want to acquire a reputation for learning at
a cheap rate, it is best to ignore the dull and
stupid knowledge which is everybody's possession and concentrate on something odd
and out of the way. Instead of quoting
Virgil quote Sidonius Apollinaris, and express loudly your contempt of those who
prefer the court poet of Augustus to the
panegyrist of Avitus, Majorianus and An-
themius. When the conversation turns on
Jane Eyre or *Wuthering Heights* (which of
course you have not read) say you infinitely
prefer *The Tenant of Wildfell Hall*. When
Donne is praised, pooh-pooh him and tell the
praiser that he should read Gongora. At the
mention of Raphael, make as though to
vomit outright (though you have never been
inside the Vatican); the Raphael Mengses
at Petersburg, you will say, are the only
tolerable paintings. In this way you will

173

get the reputation of a person of profound learning and the most exquisite taste. Whereas, if you give proof of knowing your Dickens, of having read the Bible, the English classics, Euclid and Horace, nobody will think anything of you at all. You will be just like everybody else.

The extreme inadequacy of my education has often led me, in the course of my journalistic career, to adopt these tactics. I have written airily of the remote and odd in order to conceal my ignorance of the near and the classical. The profession of a literary journalist is not one that greatly encourages honesty. Everything conspires to make him a charlatan. He has no leisure to read regularly or with purpose; at the same time reviewing makes him acquainted with a mass of fragmentary and miscellaneous information. He would be a prodigy of intellectual integrity if he did not reproduce it in his own articles, casually and with confidence, as though each queer item were an outlying promontory of the vast continent of his universal knowledge. Moreover the necessity under which he labours of always being readable tempts him at all costs to be original and unusual. Is it to be wondered at if, knowing five lines each of Virgil and Apollinaris, he prefers to quote the latter? Or if, knowing none of Virgil, he turns his ignorance into a critical virtue and lets it be understood that the best minds have now gone on from Maro to Sidonius?

In the monastery of Subiaco, which lies in that remote back of beyond behind Tivoli, there are, among many other things of beauty and historical interest, a number of frescoes by a thirteenth-century master, unknown except as the author of these works, called Conxolus. The name is superb and could not be improved. Majestic and at the same time slightly grotesque, uncommon (indeed, for all I know, unique) and easily memorable, it is a name which seems by right to belong to a great man. Conxolus: at the sound of those rich syllables the cultured person has a vague uncomfortable feeling that he ought to know what they connote. Is it a battle? or scholastic philosophy? or a heresy? or what? Learning, after a moment's agonizing suspense (during which he is uncertain whether his interlocutor will let out the secret or force him to confess his ignorance) that Conxolus was a painter, the cultured person confidently plunges. "Such a *mar*vellous artist!" he rapturously exclaims.

The old journalistic Adam is not quite dead within me, and I know my cultured

society.   The temptation was strong.   I
would preach Conxolus to a benighted world
and, exalting him as an artist, exalt myself
at the same time as an art critic.   And how
cheaply!   For the price of three gallons of
petrol, ten francs of post-cards and tips, and
an excellent lunch, with trout, at Tivoli, I
should have made myself completely master
of my subject and established my *Kunstforscher's* reputation.   No tiresome journeys
to far away galleries in search of the master's
minor works, no laborious reading of German monographs.   Just this one extremely
agreeable trip to the upper Anio, this forty
minutes' walk uphill, this little trot round
Saint Benedict's first hermitage—and that
was all.   I would go back to London, I
would write some articles, or even a little
book, with handsome reproductions, about
the master.   And when, in cultured society,
people talked of Duccio or Simone Martini,
I should smile from the height of my superiority.   "They are all very well, no
doubt.   But when one has seen Conxolus."
And I should go on talking of his tactile and
olfactory values, his magistral treatment of
the fourth dimension, his exquisitely subtle
use of *repoussoirs* and that extraordinary
mastery of colour which enabled him to paint
all the flesh in his pictures in two tones of

ochre, impure purple and goose-turd green. And my auditors (terrified, as all the frequenters of cultured society always are, of being left behind in the intellectual race), would listen with grave avidity. And they would leave me, triumphantly conscious that they had scored a point over their rivals, that they had entered a new swim from which all but the extremely select were excluded, that their minds were dressed in a fashion that came straight from Paris (for of course I should give them to understand that Derain and Matisse entirely agreed with me); and from that day forth the name of Conxolus, and with it my name, would begin to reverberate, *crescendo*, with an ever-growing rumour of admiration, in all the best drawing-rooms, from Euston to the World's End.

The temptation was strong; but I wrestled with it heroically and at last had the mastery. I decided that I would not pervert the truth for the sake of any reputation, however flattering, for critical insight and discrimination. For the truth, alas, is that our unique and high-sounding Conxolus is an entirely negligible painter. Competent and well-trained; but no more. His principal merit consists in the fact that he lived in the thirteenth century and worked in the characteristic style of his period. He painted in the decadent Byzantine manner which we, arguing backwards from sixteenth-century Florence instead of forwards from sixth-century Ravenna, miscall "primitive." It is in this, I repeat, that his principal merit consists—at any rate for us. For a century ago his primitiveness would only have aroused derision and pity. We have changed all that nowadays; and so thoroughly that there are many young people who, in their anxiety not to be thought old-fashioned, regard all pictures bearing a close resemblance to their subjects as highly suspicious and, unless guaranteed chemically pure by some recognized æsthetic authority, *a priori* ridiculous. To these ascetics all natural beauty, when reproduced by art, is damnable. A beautiful woman accurately painted is "chocolate boxy"; a beautiful landscape mere poetry. If a work of art is obviously charming, if it moves at first sight, then, according to these people, it must also necessarily be bad. This doctrine applied to music has led to the exaltation of Bach, even Bach in his most mechanical and soulless moments, at the expense of Beethoven. It has led to the dry "classical" way of playing Mozart, who is supposed to be unemotional because he is not vulgarly emotional, like Wagner. It has led to steam organ-like performances of Handel and senseless bellowings of Palestrina. And the absurd young, in reaction against the sentimentalities and lachrymose idealisms which they imagine to have characterized the later Victorian age, being left absolutely unmoved by these performances, have for that very reason applauded them as in the highest degree artistic. It is the same in painting. The muddier the colours, the more distorted the figures, the higher the art. There are hundreds of young painters who dare not paint realistically and charmingly, even if they could, for fear of losing the esteem of the young connoisseurs who are their patrons. True, good painters paint well and express all they have to say whatever convention they may use; and indifferent painters paint indifferently in all circumstances. It ought, therefore, to give us no concern whatever if indifferent young painters do prefer distortion and muddy colouring to gaiety, realism and charm. It does not seriously matter how they paint. At the same time the world did get a certain amount of entertainment out of its indifferent painters in the past, when they did their best to imitate nature and tell stories. It got faithful copies of beautiful objects, it got documents and pictorial notes, it got amusing anecdotes and comments on life. These things might not be great pictures; but they were at any rate worth something, for they had an other than æsthetic value. Aiming as he does at some mythical ideal of pure æstheticism, to which all but form is sacrificed, the young talent-less painter of the present time gives us nothing but boredom. For his pictures are not good pictures, and they do not make amends for their badness by reminding us of pleasing objects; they have not even the merit of being documents or comments, they do not even tell a story. In a word they have nothing to recommend them. From being an entertainer, the second-rate artist (if he happens also to be "advanced") has become an intolerable bore.

The young's mistrust of realism does not apply only to contemporary art; it is also retrospective. Of two equally untalented artists of the past youth unhesitatingly prefers the man who is least realistic, most "primitive." Conxolus is admired above his seventeenth-century counterpart, simply because his figures remind one of nothing that is charming in nature, because he is innocent of light and shade, because the composition is rigidly symmetrical and because the emotional content of his ardently Christian pictures has, for us, completely evaporated, leaving nothing that can evoke in our bosoms the slightest sentiment of any kind, with the single exception of those famous æsthetic emotions which the young so studiously cultivate.

True, the convention in which the seventeenth-century Italian painters worked was an intolerable one. The wild gesticulations with which they filled their pictures, in the hope of artificially creating an atmosphere of passion, is fundamentally ludicrous. The baroque style and the kindred romantic style are the two styles best fitted in the nature of things for the expression of comedy. Aristophanes, Rabelais, Nashe, Balzac, Dickens, Rowlandson, Goya, Doré, Daumier and the nameless makers of grotesques all over the world and at every period—all practitioners of pure comedy, whether in literature or in art—have employed an extravagant, baroque, romantic style. Naturally; for pure comedy it is essentially extravagant and enormous. Except in the hands of prodigious men of genius (such as Marlowe and Shakespeare, Michelangelo and Rembrandt) this style, when used for serious purposes, is ludicrous. Almost all baroque art and almost all the kindred romantic art of a later epoch are grotesque because the artists (not of the first order) are trying to express something tragic in terms of a style essentially comic. In this respect the works of the "primitives"—even of the second-rate primitives—are really preferable to the works of their *seicento* descendants. For in their pictures there is no fundamental incongruity between the style and subject. But this is a negative quality; second-rate primitives are decent but they are extraordinarily dull. The work of the later realists may be vulgar and absurd as a whole; but it is redeemed, very often, by the charm of its details. You can find, in the pictures of second-rate artists of the seventeenth century, charming landscapes, interesting physiognomies, studies of curious effects of light and shade—things which do nothing, it is true, to redeem these works, viewed as wholes, from badness, but are nevertheless agreeable and interesting in themselves. In the Conxoluses of an earlier epoch the work as a whole is respectable; but its dulness is not relieved by any curious or delightful details. By their absurdly ascetic distrust of the obviously delightful, the young have deprived themselves of a great deal of pleasure. They bore themselves by second-rate Conxoluses when they might amuse themselves by equally second-rate Fetis and Caravaggios and Rosa da Tivolis and Carpionis and Guercinos and Luca

Giordanos and all the rest of them. If one must look at second-rate pictures at all— and there are so few good pictures that one inevitably must—it is surely more reasonable to look at those which give one something (even though the plums be embedded in a suet of horror) than those which give one absolutely nothing at all.

BORGO SAN SEPOLCRO is not very easy to get at. There is a small low-comedy railway across the hills from Arezzo. Or you can approach it up the Tiber valley from Perugia. Or, if you happen to be at Urbino, there is a motor 'bus which takes you to San Sepolcro, up and down through the Apennines, in something over seven hours. No joke, that journey, as I know by experience. But it is worth doing, though preferably in some other vehicle than the 'bus, for the sake of the Bocca Trabaria, that most beautiful of Apennine passes, between the Tiber valley and the upper valley of the Metauro. It was in the early spring that we crossed it. Our omnibus groaned and rattled slowly up a bleak northern slope, among bald rocks, withered grass and still unbudded trees. It crossed the *col* and suddenly, as though by a miracle, the ground was yellow with innumerable primroses, each flower a little emblem of the sun that had called it into being.

And when at last one has arrived at San Sepolcro, what is there to be seen? A little town surrounded by walls, set in a broad flat valley between hills; some fine Renaissance palaces with pretty balconies of wrought iron; a not very interesting church, and finally, the best picture in the world.

The best picture in the world is painted in fresco on the wall of a room in the town hall. Some unwittingly beneficent vandal had it covered, some time after it was painted, with a thick layer of plaster, under which it lay hidden for a century or two, to be revealed at last in a state of preservation remarkably perfect for a fresco of its date. Thanks to the vandals, the visitor who now enters the Palazzo dei Conservatori at Borgo San Sepolcro finds the stupendous Resurrection almost as Piero della Francesca left it. Its clear, yet subtly sober colours shine out from the wall with scarcely impaired freshness. Damp has blotted out nothing of the design, nor dirt obscured it. We need no imagination to help us figure forth its beauty; it stands there before us in entire and actual splendour, the greatest picture in the world.

The greatest picture in the world. . . . You smile. The expression is ludicrous, of course. Nothing is more futile than the occupation of those connoisseurs who spend their time compiling first and second elevens

of the world's best painters, eights and fours
of musicians, fifteens of poets, all-star
troupes of architects and so on. Nothing is
so futile because there are a great many
kinds of merit and an infinite variety of
human beings. Is Fra Angelico a better
artist than Rubens? Such questions, you insist, are meaningless. It is all a matter of
personal taste. And up to a point this is
true. But there does exist, none the less,
an absolute standard of artistic merit. And
it is a standard which is in the last resort a
moral one. Whether a work of art is good
or bad depends entirely on the quality of
the character which expresses itself in the
work. Not that all virtuous men are good
artists, nor all artists conventionally virtuous. Longfellow was a bad poet, while
Beethoven's dealings with his publishers
were frankly dishonourable. But one can
be dishonourable towards one's publishers
and yet preserve the kind of virtue that is
necessary to a good artist. That virtue is
the virtue of integrity, of honesty towards
oneself. Bad art is of two sorts: that which
is merely dull, stupid and incompetent, the
negatively bad; and the positively bad,
which is a lie and a sham. Very often the
lie is so well told that almost every one is
taken in by it—for a time. In the end, how-

ever, lies are always found out. Fashion changes, the public learns to look with a different focus and, where a little while ago it saw an admirable work which actually moved its emotions, it now sees a sham. In the history of the arts we find innumerable shams of this kind, once taken as genuine, now seen to be false. The very names of most of them are now forgotten. Still, a dim rumour that Ossian once was read, that Bulwer was thought a great novelist and "Festus" Bailey a mighty poet still faintly reverberates. Their counterparts are busily earning praise and money at the present day. I often wonder if I am one of them. It is impossible to know. For one can be an artistic swindler without meaning to cheat and in the teeth of the most ardent desire to be honest.

Sometimes the charlatan is also a first-rate man of genius and then you have such strange artists as Wagner and Bernini, who can turn what is false and theatrical into something almost sublime.

That it is difficult to tell the genuine from the sham is proved by the fact that enormous numbers of people have made mistakes and continue to make them. Genuineness, as I have said, always triumphs in the long run. But at any given moment the majority of people, if they do not actually prefer the sham to the real, at least like it as much, paying an indiscriminate homage to both.

And now, after this little digression we can return to San Sepolcro and the greatest picture in the world. Great it is, absolutely great, because the man who painted it was genuinely noble as well as talented. And to me personally the most moving of pictures, because its author possessed almost more than any other painter those qualities of character which I most admire and because his purely æsthetic preoccupations are of a kind which I am by nature best fitted to understand. A natural, spontaneous, and unpretentious grandeur—this is the leading quality of all Piero's work. He is majestic without being at all strained, theatrical or hysterical—as Handel is majestic, not as Wagner. He achieves grandeur naturally with every gesture he makes, never consciously strains after it. Like Alberti, with whose architecture, as I hope to show, his painting has certain affinities, Piero seems to have been inspired by what I may call the religion of Plutarch's *Lives*—which is not Christianity, but a worship of what is admirable in man. Even his technically religious pictures are pæans in praise of human dignity. And he is everywhere intellectual.

With the drama of life and religion he is very little concerned. His battle pictures at Arezzo are not dramatic compositions in spite of the many dramatic incidents they contain. All the turmoil, all the emotions of the scenes have been digested by the mind into a grave intellectual whole. It is as though Bach had written the 1812 Overture. Nor are the two superb pictures in the National Gallery—the Nativity and the Baptism—distinguished for any particular sympathy with the religious or emotional significance of the events portrayed. In the extraordinary Flagellation at Urbino, the nominal subject of the picture recedes into the background on the left-hand side of the panel, where it serves to balance the three mysterious figures standing aloof in the right foreground. We seem to have nothing here but an experiment in composition, but an experiment so strange and so startlingly successful that we do not regret the absence of dramatic significance and are entirely satisfied. The Resurrection at San Sepolcro is more dramatic. Piero has made the simple triangular composition symbolic of the subject. The base of the triangle is formed by the sepulchre; and the soldiers sleeping round it are made to indicate by their position the upward jet of the two sides, which meet at the apex in the face of the risen Christ, who is standing, a banner in his right hand, his left foot already raised and planted on the brim of the sepulchre, preparing to set out into the world. No geometrical arrangement could have been more simple or more apt. But the being who rises before our eyes from the tomb is more like a Plutarchian hero than the Christ of conventional religion. The body is perfectly developed, like that of a Greek athlete; so formidably strong that the wound in its muscular flank seems somehow an irrelevance. The face is stern and pensive, the eyes cold. The whole figure is expressive of physical and intellectual power. It is the resurrection of the classical ideal, incredibly much grander and more beautiful than the classical reality, from the tomb where it had lain so many hundred years.

Æsthetically, Piero's work has this resemblance to Alberti's: that it too is essentially an affair of masses. What Alberti is to Brunelleschi, Piero della Francesca is to his contemporary, Botticelli. Botticelli was fundamentally a draughtsman, a maker of supple and resilient lines, thinking in terms of arabesques inscribed on the flat. Piero, on the contrary, has a passion for solidity as such. There is something in all his works that reminds one constantly of Egyptian sculpture. Piero has that Egyptian love of the smooth rounded surface that is the external symbol and expression of a mass. The faces of his personages look as though they were carved out of some very hard rock into which it had been impossible to engrave the details of a human physiognomy—the hollows, the lines and wrinkles of real life. They are ideal, like the faces of Egyptian gods and princes, surface meeting and marrying with curved unbroken surface in an almost geometrical fashion. Look, for example, at the faces of the women in Piero's fresco at Arezzo: "The Queen of Sheba recognizing the Holy Tree." They are all of one peculiar cast: the foreheads are high, rounded and smooth; the necks are like cylinders of polished ivory; from the midst of the concave sockets the eyelids swell out in one uninterrupted curve into convexity; the cheeks are unbrokenly smooth and the subtle curvature of their surfaces is indicated by a very delicate chiaroscuro which suggests more powerfully the solidity and mass of the flesh than the most spectacular Caravaggioesque light and shade could do.

Piero's passion for solidity betrays itself no less strikingly in his handling of the dresses and drapery of his figures. It is noticeable, for example, that wherever the subject permits, he makes his personages appear in curious head-dresses that remind one by their solid geometrical qualities of those oddly-shaped ceremonial hats or tiaras worn by the statues of Egyptian kings. Among the frescoes at Arezzo are several which illustrate this peculiarity. In that representing Heraclius restoring the True Cross to Jerusalem, all the ecclesiastical dignitaries are wearing enormously high head-dresses, conical, trumpet-shaped, even rectangular. They are painted very smoothly with, it is obvious, a profound relish for their solidity. One or two similar head-dresses, with many varieties of wonderfully rounded helmets are lovingly represented in the battle-pieces in the same place. The Duke of Urbino, in the well-known portrait at the Uffizi, is wearing a red cloth cap whose shape is somewhat like that of the "Brodrick" of the modern English soldier, but without the peak— a cylinder fitting round the head, topped by a projecting disk as the crown. Its smoothness and the roundness of its surfaces are emphasized in the picture. Nor does Piero neglect the veils of his female figures. Though transparent and of lawn, they hang round the heads of his women in stiff folds, as though they were made of steel. Among clothes he has a special fondness for pleated bodices and tunics. The bulge and recession of the pleated stuff fascinates him and he likes to trace the way in which the fluted folds follow the curve of the body beneath. To drapery he gives, as we might expect, a particular weight and richness. Perhaps his most exquisite handling of drapery is to be seen in the altar-piece of the Madonna della Misericordia, which now hangs near the Resurrection in the town hall at San Sepolcro. The central figure in this picture, which is one of the earliest of Piero's extant works, represents the Virgin, standing, and stretching out her arms, so as to cover two groups of suppliants on either side with the folds of her heavy blue mantle. The mantle and the Virgin's dress hang in simple perpendicular folds, like the flutings on the robe of the archaic bronze charioteer at the Louvre. Piero has painted these alternately convex and concave surfaces with a peculiar gusto.

It is not my intention to write a treatise on Piero della Francesca; that has been done sufficiently often and sufficiently badly to make it unnecessary for me to bury that consummate artist any deeper under layers of muddy comment. All I have meant to do in this place is to give the reasons why I like his works and my justifications for calling

the Resurrection the greatest picture in the
world.   I am attracted to his character by
his intellectual power; by his capacity for
unaffectedly making the grand and noble
gesture; by his pride in whatever is splendid
in humanity.   And in the artist I find peculiarly sympathetic the lover of solidity, the
painter of smooth curving surfaces, the composer who builds with masses.   For myself
I prefer him to Botticelli, so much so indeed,
that if it were necessary to sacrifice all Botticelli's works in order to save the Resurrection, the Nativity, the Madonna della
Misericordia and the Arezzo frescoes, I
should unhesitatingly commit the Primavera
and all the rest of them to the flames.   It is
unfortunate for Piero's reputation that his
works should be comparatively few and in
most cases rather difficult of access.   With
the exception of the Nativity and Baptism
at the National Gallery, all the really important works of Piero are at Arezzo, San
Sepolcro and Urbino.   The portraits of the
Duke and Duchess of Urbino with their respective triumphs, in the Uffizi, are charming and exceedingly "amusing"; but they do
not represent Piero at his best.   The altar-
piece at Perugia and the Madonna with
saints and donor at Milan are neither of
them first-rate.   The St. Jerome at Venice

is goodish; so too is the damaged fresco of the Malatesta, at Rimini. The Louvre possesses nothing and Germany can only boast of a study of architecture, inferior to that at Urbino. Anybody, therefore, who wants to know Piero, must go from London to Arezzo, San Sepolcro and Urbino. Now Arezzo is a boring sort of town, and so ungrateful to its distinguished sons that there is no monument within its walls to the divine Aretino. I deplore Arezzo; but to Arezzo, nevertheless, you must go to see Piero's most considerable works. From Arezzo you must make your way to San Sepolcro, where the inn is only just tolerable, and to which the means of communication are so bad that, unless you come in your own car, you are fairly compelled to stay there. And from San Sepolcro you must travel by 'bus for seven hours across the Apennines to Urbino. Here, it is true, you have not only two admirable Pieros (the Flagellation and an architectural scene), but the most exquisite palace in Italy and very nearly a good hotel. Even on the most wearily reluctant tourist Urbino imposes itself; there is no escaping it; it must be seen. But in the case of Arezzo and San Sepolcro there is no such moral compulsion. Few tourists, in consequence, take the trouble to visit them.

If the principal works of Piero were to be seen in Florence, and those of Botticelli at San Sepolcro I do not doubt that the public estimation of these two masters would be reversed.   Artistic English spinsters would stand in rapturous contemplation before the story of the True Cross, instead of before the Primavera.   Raptures depend largely upon the stars in Baedeker, and the stars are more freely distributed to works of art in accessible towns than to those in the inaccessible.   If the Arena chapel were in the mountains of Calabria, instead of at Padua, we should all have heard a good deal less of Giotto.

But enough.   The shade of Conxolus rises up to remind me that I am running into the error of those who measure merit by a scale of oddness and rarity.

THE PIERIAN SPRING

"A LITTLE learning," said Pope, "is a dangerous thing." And who, indeed, should have known its dangers more intimately than the man who had undertaken to translate Homer without (for all practical purposes) knowing a word of Greek? "Drink deep"—the exhortation, you feel, comes from the translator's very heart—"or taste not the Pierian spring."

Drink deep. The advice is good, provided always that the liquor be a sound one. But is the Pierian spring sound? That is the question. Not all medicinal waters are good for every drinker. People who can profitably drink deep of Carlsbad or Montecatini may die of a surfeit of Bath. Similarly the Pierian spring is not for everybody. The philosopher and the man of science may drink of it as deeply as they like and it will do them nothing but good. To the poet it can certainly do no harm; his native woodnotes are enriched by a little learning. The politician would do well to drink of this spring more often and more copiously than he actually does. The man of business may

find profit in the draught, while the dilettante drinks for mere pleasure. But there is
at least one class of men to whom the Pierian
spring seems to be almost fatal. On no
account should the artist be allowed to drink
of it.

Two centuries have passed since Pope
warned his readers against the dangers of a
little learning. The history of those two
centuries, and especially of the last fifty
years, has proved that, so far as the artist
is concerned, much learning is quite as dangerous as little learning. It is, in fact, a
great deal more dangerous.

I can best explain what happens when
artists drink deep of the Pierian spring by
describing a kind of Arts and Crafts exhibition which I happened to see, a summer or
two since, in Munich. It was a huge affair.
Furniture, jewellery, ceramics, textiles—
every kind of applied art was copiously represented. And all the exhibits were German.
All German—and yet these pots and pans,
these chairs and tables, these weavings,
paintings, carvings, forgings spoke a hundred languages besides the native Teuton.
Aryan, Mongolian, Semitic, Bantu, Polynesian, Maya—the stocks and stones of
Munich were fluent in all the tongues.
Here, for example, stood a Mexican pot,

decorated with Moorish arabesques; here a
statuette that was sixth-century Greek,
subtly mingled with Benin. Here was a
Black Forest peasant's table standing on
Egyptian legs; here a crucifix that might
have been carved by a T'ang artist who happened to have spent a year in Italy as the
pupil of Bernini. Goat, woman, lion and
gryphon—here were chimæras and empusas
at every turn. And none of them (that was
the real horror, for success justifies everything) none of them were good.

Germany, it is true, is the country where
the dangers of too much learning have made
themselves most apparent. It is the country
that has drunk most deeply of the Pierian
spring. For the last fifty years German publishers have brought out six illustrated monographs to every one produced in France, and
a dozen at least to every one that we have
published in England. With untiring in-
dustry and an enthusiasm which nothing—
not the War, not even the Peace—has been
able to damp, the Germans have photo-
graphed the artistic remains of every people
that has ever flourished on the face of the
earth. And they have published these photographs, with learned prefaces, in little books,
which they sold, once upon a time, for a
mark apiece, and which even now do not cost

more than, shall we say fifteen or twenty thousand millions. The Germans know more about the artistic styles of the past than any other people in the world—and their own art, to-day, is about as hopelessly dreary as any national art could well be. Its badness is, in mathematical terms, a function of its learnedness.

What has happened in Germany has happened, though to a slightly less marked degree, in every country of the world. We all know too much, and our knowledge prevents us—unless we happen to be artists of exceptional independence and talent—from doing good work.

Up till quite recently no European artist knew, or thought it worth while to know, anything about any forms of art except those which had been current in his own continent. And even of those he knew precious little. A sixteenth-century sculptor, for example, knew something about Greek carving—or something, at any rate, about Roman copies of carvings belonging to a certain period of Greek art. But of the works which the sculptors of the Gothic past had produced, even in his own country, he knew very little; and what he knew, he was disposed to deride as being merely barbarous. There were no photographs then; there were even very few engravings. The Renaissance sculptor worked in an almost total ignorance of what had been done by other sculptors, at other periods or in countries other than his own. The result was that he was able to concentrate on the one convention that seemed to him good—the classical—and work away at it undisturbed, until he had developed all its potential resources.

The case of architecture is still more remarkable. For three hundred years the classical orders reigned supreme in Europe. Gothic was forgotten and despised. Nobody knew anything of any other styles. Generation after generation of architects worked away uninterruptedly in terms of this one convention. And what an astonishing variety of achievements they were able to get out of it! Using the same elementary classical units, successive generations produced a series of absolutely original and dissimilar works. Brunelleschi, Alberti, Michelangelo, Palladio, Bernini, Pietro da Cortona, Christopher Wren, Adam, Nash—all these architects worked in the same classical convention, making it yield a series of distinctive masterpieces, each utterly unlike the other.

These were all men of genius who would have done great things in any circumstances. What is still more striking is the achieve-

ment of the minor artists.   During all this
long period the work of even a journeyman
had qualities which we look for in vain
among the lesser artists of the present time.
It was the absence of distracting knowledge
that made possible this high level of achievement among the less talented men.   There
was for them only one possible convention.
They concentrated their whole mind on getting the best they possibly could out of it.

How different is the present state of affairs!   The artist of to-day knows, and has
been taught to appreciate, the artistic conventions of every people that has ever
existed.   For him, there is no single right
convention; there are a thousand conventions, which can all claim his respect because men have produced fine works in terms
of all of them.   Gone is the blessed ignorance, vanished the healthy contempt for all
but one tradition.   There is no tradition
now, or there are a hundred traditions—it
comes to the same thing.   The artist's
knowledge tends to distract him, to dissipate
his energies.   Instead of spending his whole
life systematically exploiting one convention, he moves restlessly among all the
known styles, undecided which to work in,
borrowing hints from each.

But in art there are no short cuts to successful achievement. You cannot acquire in half an hour the secrets of a style which it has taken the work of generations to refine to its perfection. In half an hour, it is true, you can learn what are the most striking superficial characteristics of the style; you can learn to caricature it. That is all. To understand a style you must give yourself up to it; you must live, so to speak, inside it; you must concentrate and steadily labour.

But concentration is precisely the thing which excessive knowledge tends to render impossible—for all, at any rate, but the most individually gifted, the most strong-minded of artists. They, it is true, can be left to look after themselves. Whatever their mental and physical environment, they will be themselves. Knowledge has had its most disastrous effects on the minor men, on the rank and file. These, in another century, would have worked away undistracted, trying to get the best out of a single convention—trying and, what is more, generally succeeding to the very limit of their natural capacities. Their descendants are trying to get the best out of fifty different conventions at once. With what results Munich most hideously shows. And not only Munich, but Paris too, London, New York, the whole knowledge-ridden world.

Still, the knowledge exists and is easily available. There is no destroying or concealing it. There can be no recapture of the old ignorance which allowed the artists of the past to go on working in one style for years, for centuries even, at a time. Knowledge has brought with it restlessness, uncertainty and the possibility of rapid and incessant change in the conventions of art. How many styles have come and gone during the last seventy years! Pre-Raphaelitism, impressionism, art nouveau, futurism, post impressionism, cubism, expressionism. It would have taken the Egyptians a hundred centuries to run through such a fortune of styles. To-day, we invent a new convention—or, more often, resuscitate a combination of old conventions out of the past—exploit it, and throw it away, all in the space of five years. The fixity of the old traditions, the sure refinement of taste, born of ignorance and intolerant fastidiousness, have gone. Will they ever return? In time, no doubt, the artists will have inured themselves to the poison of the Pierian spring. The immense mass of knowledge which, in our minds, is still crude, will gradually be digested. When that has happened, some sort of fixity—or rather some slow and steady motion, for in life there is no fixity—

will have been achieved. Meanwhile, we must be content to live in an age of dissipated energies, of experiment and *pastiche*, of restlessness and hopeless uncertainty.

The vast increase in our knowledge of art history has affected not only the artists themselves, but all those who take an interest in the arts. For *tout savoir est tout pardonner;* we have learned to appreciate and see the best in every style. To Voltaire and Dr. Johnson even Gothic art seemed a barbarism. What would they have said if we had asked them to admire the plastic beauties of a Polynesian statue, or the painting of an animal by an artist who lived millenniums before the dawn of history? Knowledge has enabled us to sympathize with unfamiliar points of view, to appreciate artistic conventions devised by people utterly unlike ourselves. All this, no doubt, is a very good thing. But our sympathy is so vast and we are so much afraid of showing ourselves intolerant towards the things we ought to like, that we have begun to love in our all-embracing way not merely the highest, in whatever convention, when we see it, but the lowest too.

We are not content with appreciating the good things which our ancestors condemned. Appetite grows with what it feeds on. The good is not enough to satisfy our hungry appreciation; we must swallow the bad as well. To justify ourselves in this appreciation of what is bad, we have created a whole series of new æsthetic values. The process which began some time ago has gone on with ever-increasing speed and thoroughness, till there is now almost nothing, however bad, from which we cannot derive pleasure.

Historically, I suppose, the first stage in the breaking up of the old standards of taste was the invention of the "picturesque." A picturesque object may be defined as a thing which has some quality or qualities in excess of the normal. The nature of the excessive quality is almost a matter of indifference. Thus, even an excess of dirtiness is sufficient to render an object picturesque. The ideally picturesque object or scene possesses several excessive qualities in violent contrast one with another—for example, excess of gloom contrasting with excess of light, excess of magnificence with excess of squalor.

The quaint may be defined as the picturesque made smaller and touched with the comic. Those little old houses which Dickens so loved to describe—all holes and corners and curious accidents—are typical pieces of quaintness. There is always something snug and homely about the quaint, something even, in a comic way, slightly virtuous—funnily good, like Tom Pinch in *Martin Chuzzlewit*. It was the Victorian middle classes who erected quaintness into a standard of æsthetic excellence. Their love of it, coupled with their love of the picturesque, permitted them to admire a vast number of things which have practically no connection with art at all. What I may call "arty-craftiness" or "peasantry" is a Tolstoyan derivation from the quaint.

The great invention of more recent years has been the "amusing." In origin this is a highly sophisticated, upper-class standard of value. All bad art, whose badness is a positive and not a merely negative quality of respectable dulness, may be said to be amusing. For instance, Wordsworth, when he writes badly, is not at all amusing. Moore, on the other hand, is; for Moore's badness is of the period, highly coloured, mannered and mincing. The badness of Wordsworth, like his goodness, is of all time. The *Ecclesiastical Sonnets* are absolute bathos, just as the finest passages in the *Prelude* and *Excursion* are absolute poetry.

A highly-developed sense of the amusing in art is now extremely common. Few of those who take any conscious interest in the arts are now without it. Amusingness has even come to have a commercial value; dealers find that they can get good prices for the *papier mâché* furniture of the eighteen-fifties, for the wax flowers and statuettes of the age of Louis-Philippe. The people who collect these objects appear to derive as much satisfaction from them—for a time at any rate—as they would from the most austerely graceful Heppelwhite or the choicest fourteenth-century ivories. And there is no reason, of course, why they should not, provided that they continue to recognize the fact that Heppelwhite is better than Victorian *papier mâché* and that mediæval ivories are more beautiful than wax flowers. But the trouble is that this recognition is not always so complete or so prompt as it should be. That is the great danger attendant on the cult of the amusing; it makes its votaries forget that there are such things as the beautiful and the sublime. In the end Erasmus Darwin comes to be preferred to Wordsworth, Longhi to Giotto. Indirectly, it is the Pierian spring that is responsible.

Part IV: By the Way

A NIGHT AT PIETRAMALA

"WHAT I love best in all the world,"
says Browning in *De Gustibus*, "is
a castle, precipice-encurled, in a gash of the
wind-grieved Apennine." *De Gustibus*, indeed. I take the hint and shall not argue
the point. Suffice it to say that, though I
like the poem, I cannot share the poet's
tastes. A castle in the Apennine would come
quite low in the list of the things I love. A
palace in Rome, a villa just outside the gates
of Siena, even a motor caravan would stand
higher. For the epithet which Browning
applies to the Apennine is only too appropriate. He himself, no doubt, enjoyed being
grieved by the wind. I can imagine him,
with bent head, tunnelling his way through
one of those hellish blasts which come hooting down, in spring and winter, through the
gashes between the hills. He would feel
exhilarated by the effort; his struggle against
the elements would elate him and he would
return to his castle to write some more than
ordinarily hearty pæan in praise of passion
and energy—passion for passion's sake,
energy admirable, not so much for its direc-

tion as for its volume. Such, I am sure, were the effects of the wind on Browning; it confirmed him in his blustering optimism. In me on the other hand, the wind of the Apennines begets nothing but neuralgia and the profoundest depression. It is not *Prospice* that I should write in the precipice-encurled castello; it is something in the style of the *City of Dreadful Night*.

That I am not exaggerating the horrors of the wind among the Apennines is proved by the fact that it has been found necessary, for the convenience and even the safety of travellers, to protect the most exposed places of the principal passes with high walls. I remember in particular one section of the main road from Florence to Bologna which is flanked for hundreds of yards by an immense parapet, like the great wall of China. The road at this point, which is between two and three thousand feet above the sea, cuts across the head of a deep and narrow valley, through which there sucks a perpetual draught. Even in summer, on halcyon days, you can hear as you pass under the lee of the wall, a melancholy wailing of the winds overhead. But on rough days in winter, in the spring and autumn, the air is full of fearful noises, as though the gates of hell had been opened and the lost souls were making holiday. What happened to travellers who passed that way before, some hundred years ago, a beneficent Grand-Ducal government built the wall, I shudder to think. They must often have been, quite literally, blown off the road.

We passed that way once in March. The Italian spring, which is not so different from the spring in other countries, was inclement that year and icy. In Florence the sun shone fitfully between huge clouds. Snow still lay, in patches on Monte Morello. The breeze was nipping. "Are the passes free of snow?" we asked at the garage where we stopped to fill our petrol tank. Animated by that typically Italian desire to give an answer that will please the questioner, the garage man assured us that the road was perfectly clear. And he said it with such conviction that we imagined, as northerners would naturally imagine, that he knew. Nothing is more charming than southern courtesy, southern sympathy and the southern desire to please. The heart is touched by the kindly interest which the Italians take in your affairs; you love them for their courteous inquisitiveness; they make you at home immediately, treat you at once as a human being and do their best to please you. It is delightful. But sometimes they are really too sympathetic

by half. For in order not to contradict you
or give you a moment's pain by disputing
the accuracy of your ideas, they will tell you
what you want to hear rather than what it
would be of real use to you to hear. At the
same time their own self-esteem will not
permit them to confess a blank ignorance;
so that they will rather tell you something
incorrect than tell you nothing at all. Thus,
when the garage man told us that there was
no snow on the road from Florence to
Bologna, he said so first, because he saw
that we wanted to go to Bologna and that
we should have been disappointed if it had
been impossible and, second, because it was
pleasanter for him to say "No snow" with
conviction than confess (which was the
truth) that he hadn't the faintest notion
whether there was snow or not.

We believed him and set out. The road
rises steeply from Florence, climbs to twelve
or fifteen hundred feet and then plunges
down again into that long flat-bottomed
valley locked in the midst of the hills, the
Mugello. By the time we had reached it
the sun had entirely disappeared, and the
sky above us was one vast yellowish-white
snowcloud. Looking at the various castelli
one passes by the way, I found Browning's

predilections more than ever incomprehensible.

Between Florence and Bologna there are two passes: the Futa and, five or six miles further on, the pass of Raticosa. It is near the top of the Futa that the Grand Dukes built the bulwark against the wind. It was strengthened, that day, by heaps of driven snow. Below and above, the slopes were deep in snow. In the midst of all this whiteness the road wound onwards and upwards like a muddy snake.

Under the lee of the wall we halted and took photographs of the Italian scenery. The air was calm where we stood and seemed in its stillness almost warm. But just above us, on a level with the top of the wall, was the wind. The snowflakes that it carried made its speed visible. It filled the ears with sound. I was reminded, as I stood there, of a rather ludicrous and deplorable version of *David Copperfield*, which Beerbohm Tree used sometimes to stage at His Majesty's. Tree himself acted two parts—Micawber and Peggotty; the former, I may add parenthetically, very well indeed (for he was an admirable comedian) the latter, in his more pathetic manner, with less success. But let that pass. Dressed as Peggotty, Tree never

made an entrance without the wind; it was
in the bluff nautical part.   Every time he
opened the door of his ship cottage on the
sands of Yarmouth there came from the
outer darkness a noise like the witches' sab-
bath.   It never blew less than a full gale
during the whole run of *David Copperfield*.
Whoo-oo-oo-oo-oo—crescendo and decres-
cendo.   In the dress circle ladies reached
for their furs, men turned up the collars of
their coats.   It was horrible.   I had hoped
then that I should never hear a wind like
that outside His Majesty's.   And I never
did till that icy March day when we paused
beneath the Grand-Ducal wall on the road
from Florence to Bologna.   There, for the
first time, I heard nature rivalling Sir Her-
bert's art.   A perfect site, I reflected, for the
Castello Browning.

At Pietramala, which lies just under the
pass of the Raticosa, we stopped at the little
inn for lunch.   The idlers who gathered immediately and as though by magic round our
machine—for even at Pietramala, even in
the snow, there were leisured car-fanciers to
whom the arrival of a ten horse power
Citroen was an event—lost no time in telling us that the road on the further side of
the pass was blocked with wind-driven
snow.   We went in to our lunch feeling a

little depressed—a little annoyed, too, with
the garage man at Florence. The inn-keeper,
however, was reassuring; gangs of men, he
told us, were to be sent out as soon as the
dinner hour was over from Pietramala and
the village on the other side of the pass. By
four o'clock the road would be clear; we
should be in Bologna before dark. When
we asked if the road by Firenzuola and
Imola were open, he shook his head. For
the second time that day we believed.

The inn-keeper's motives for not telling
the truth were different from those that ac-
tuated the man at the garage. For the latter
had lied out of misplaced politeness and
pride; the inn-keeper on the contrary, lied
merely out of self-interest. He wanted to
make us stay the night. He was perfectly
successful. At four o'clock we set out. At
the top of the pass the snow lay a yard deep
across the road, and there was not a shoveller
to be seen. We returned. The inn-keeper
was astonished: what, no shovellers? He
could hardly believe it. But to-morrow
morning the road would infallibly be
cleared. We decided to stay the night.

I had taken with me on that journey the
second volume of the *Encyclopædia Britannica*—And.-Aus. It is a capital volume
from which one can derive much useful

knowledge about Angiosperms, the Anglican Communion, Angling, Anthrax, Aphasia, Apples, Arrowroot, Asia, Aurora Borealis and Australia, not to mention Anthropology, Archeology, Architecture, Art, Astrology and Astronomy. I started hopefully on Animal Worship. "The bear," I learned, "enjoys a large measure of respect from all savage races that come in contact with it." From me, that evening, he got a large measure of envy. I thought of Mr. Belloc's rhyme:

> The Polar bear is unaware
> Of cold that stabs us through.
> For why, he has a coat of hair,
> I would I had one too.

For in spite of the fire, in spite of great-coats, it was appallingly cold. "The products of the cow," I read on, and was charmed by the compendious euphemism, "are important in magic." But I got no further; it was too cold even to read. To this day I remain ignorant of the feelings of the Thlinkit Indians towards the cow, of the Kalangs towards the dog and the Siamese towards white elephants. And if I do happen to know that the Hottentot god, Cagn, is incarnated in the praying mantis,

Ngo, that is due to the fact that I took the
same volume with me on another tour during the summer, when the evenings were less
inclement and the mind was free to devote
itself to higher things than the problem of
mere self-preservation.

It was cold enough in the sitting-room;
but the horror only really began when we
went to bed. For the bedrooms of the inn
were without fireplaces; there was no possibility of heating them. In those bedrooms
one could have preserved mutton indefinitely. Still dressed in all the woolly garments we possessed, we got into our stony
beds. Outside the wind continued to howl
among the hills. While the sheets were yet
unthawed, sleep was out of the question. I
lay awake listening to the noise of the wind
and wondering what would be the effect of
the hurricane on those flaming jets of natural
gas for which Pietramala is renowned.
Would the wind blow out those giant will-
o'-the-wisps? Or would they burn on in
spite of it? The thought of flames was
comforting; I dwelt on them with a certain
complaisance.

They are not uncommon, these jets of
fire, among the northern Apennines. Salso-
maggiore, for example, owes its coat of arms,
a salamander among the flames, to its foun-

tains of natural gas. It is in this gaseous
form alone that the hydrocarbons of the
Apennines make their appearance at the
centre of the chain. On the outer slopes
they are to be found in the more commer-
cially useful form of petroleum, which is
now extracted in small quantities from the
foothills in the neighbourhood of Piacenza,
Reggio and Modena. Who knows, we may
yet live to see the towers of Canossa rivalled
by the wooden castles of the derricks on the
slopes below.

The shutters rattled, the wind howled.
Decidedly, no fire could burn in the teeth of
such a blast. Poor *ignes fatui!* how welcome we should have made them in this ice-
house! How tenderly, like vestals, we
should have cherished any flame, however
fatuous!

From thinking of those flames and wishing that I had them in the room with me,
I went on to wonder why it was that the gas-
fires of Pietramala should be so oddly familiar to me. Had I read about them?
Had I recently heard them mentioned in conversation, or what? I racked my brains.
And then suddenly I remembered; it was in
Bence Jones's *Life and Letters of Faraday*
that I had read of Pietramala.

One very wet day in the autumn of 1814

two rather queer English tourists alighted
from their chaise in this squalid little village
of Pietramala. One was approaching middle
age, the other still a very young man. Their
names were Sir Humphry Davy and Michael
Faraday. They had been out of England
almost exactly a year. For it was in the
year 1813, just before the news of the battle
of Leipzig had reached Paris, that they
crossed into France. To us it seems in the
natural order of things that science and religion should be national affairs, that clergy-
men should scream "Hurrah and Halle-
lujah" and chemists cheer for the flag and
H_2SO_4. But it was not always so. God
and the works of God were once considered
international. God was the first to be na-
tionalized; after the Reformation he once
more became frankly tribal. But science
and even art were still above patriotism.
During the eighteenth century France and
England exchanged ideas almost as freely
as cannon balls. French scientific expedi-
tions were allowed to pass in safety between
the English fleets; Sterne was welcomed en-
thusiastically by his country's enemies. The
tradition lingered on even into the eighteen
hundreds. Napoleon gave medals to English men of science; and when, in 1813, Sir
Humphry Davy asked for leave to travel

on the continent, his request was granted at once. He was received in Paris with the highest honours, was made a member of the Institute, and in spite of the intolerable rudeness and arrogance which he habitually displayed, he was treated throughout his stay in France with the most perfect courtesy. In our more enlightened twentieth century he would have been shot as a spy or interned.

Restless and erratic, Davy hurried across Europe in search of scientific truth. All was fish that came to his net. At Genoa he made electric experiments on the torpedo fish. At Florence he borrowed the great burning-glass of the Grand Dukes and, with its aid, set a diamond on fire. At Rome he analysed the pigments employed by the artists of antiquity. At Naples he made experiments on iodine and excursions up Vesuvius. With him went Michael Faraday as "assistant in experiments and writing." Lady Davy, however, tried to use him as courier and confidential servant as well. Young Faraday found the position a little trying. It was only the consciousness that he was being given an unrivalled opportunity to educate himself that decided him to keep his post. Sir Humphry's character might not be entirely estimable; (indeed, Faraday was known to remark in later years that "the

greatest of all his great advantages was
that he had had, in Davy, a model to teach
him what he should avoid"); but he was,
undoubtedly, a mine of scientific learning.
To be with him constantly, as Faraday was,
during those eighteen months of travel, was
a liberal education. Young Faraday knew
it and put up with Lady D.

At Pietramala, then, they stopped in the
pouring rain—and doubtless in the howling
wind as well—to look at the natural fire-
works. Specimens of the gas were bottled
and taken down to Florence for analysis.
Sir Humphry concluded, correctly, that it
was a light hydrocarburet, pure.

To this desolate little village on the crest
of the Apennines Faraday devotes a couple
of pages in his journal. To Florence, except
in so far as it was a town where there were
facilities for making experiments, he gives
no space at all. Faraday paid little attention to the works of man, however beautiful. It was the works of God that interested him. There is a magnificent con-
sistency about him. All that he writes in
his journal or letters is perfectly in character. He is always the natural philosopher.
To discover truth is his sole aim and interest.
His purpose is unalterably fixed. He never
allows himself to be distracted—not by art,

which he almost completely ignores; not by politics which, in the tremendous closing scenes of the Napoleonic drama he mentions casually once or twice, not at all by the delights of casual social intercourse, though he always found time for friendship—but pursues his course steadily, perseverantly, modestly, disinterestedly and withal triumphantly as a conquering man of genius.

Outside science his great interest was religion. The battle between science and dogmatic theology, which was waged during the latter half of the nineteenth century created an impression, which still survives, that there is a certain radical incompatibility between science and religion. History shows that, as a matter of fact, no such incompatibility exists. If we read the biographies of the three most genial (in the French sense), men of science that England has produced—Sir Isaac Newton, Faraday and James Clerk Maxwell—we shall find that all three were profoundly religious. Sir Isaac devoted the greater part of a long life to the interpretation of Biblical prophecy. Faraday was an earnest and ardent Christian of the Sandemanian sect. Clerk Maxwell was a great mystic as well as a great man of science; there are letters of his which show him to have been of the company of Boehme and Swedenborg (himself, by the way, a scientific man of great distinction). There is nothing in all this that should surprise us. "An infidel astronomer is mad"; tempered, this piece of rhetoric is something like a truth. For it is certainly impossible to study nature at all closely without becoming convinced of the extraordinary strangeness and mysteriousness of the familiar world in which the mass of human beings unquestioningly pass their lives. The further our knowledge extends and the more completely we realise its implications, the more mysterious this universe is seen to be. A man must be crass and unimaginative indeed if he can study the intricacies of life, the movements of the stars, the intimate constitution of matter without feeling from time to time a sense of awe and amazement. In the ranks of the professional scientists such men undoubtedly find their place; there are unimaginative men in all professions, from that of the jockey to that of the bishop. But they are not, in general, the best at their jobs. Without imagination, without sensitiveness it is impossible to be a successful man of science. It would be difficult to find any great scientific man who had not been touched by this sense of wonder at the strangeness of things. It betrays itself in

different ways according to the upbringing
and temperament of those who feel it.   In
some, as quiet and orthodox religion; in
others, unwilling to commit themselves definitely about the nature of the mystery which
surrounds them, as agnosticism; in others
again (Clerk Maxwell and Swedenborg are
examples) the man of science is endowed
with the peculiar mental qualities of the
mystic; in yet other cases we find men possessing these same mystical qualities, but
unrefined and somehow coarse (for there are
good mystics and poor mystics just as there
are good and poor artists), and then we have,
not Clerk Maxwell with his delicate and
beautiful mysticism, but Newton the interpreter of the prophetic books.   For Faraday
the corollary and complement of science was
protestant Christianity.   His sense of wonder, his awe in face of the beautiful mystery
of the world, expressed itself in the terms of
Sandemanian meetings and Bible reading.
He stands in the scale of mystics somewhere
about half-way between Maxwell and Newton, not very highly gifted but at the same
time not vulgarly gifted, a sort of Andrea
del Sarto between Giotto on the one hand
and Caravaggio on the other.   A Cherubini
between Mozart and Strauss.

That king who, in Anatole France's fable

was only to be cured of his melancholy by
putting on the shirt of a happy man, would
have been well advised to apply to Faraday.
A shirt of his would have been specific
against the king's malady. For if any man
was happy it was surely he. All his life
long he did, professionally, the things he desired to do. To know, to discover the truth
—that was his desire. And it is a desire
whose fulfilment does not lead to disappointment and boredom, as does the fulfilment of
almost every other human longing. For
there is no end to truth; each part of it
reveals, when found, yet other parts to be
discovered. The man who desires knowledge knows no satiety, for the knowable is
perpetually new. He might live innumerable lives and never grow weary. True, the
knowable world is not everything. There is
also the world of feelings; there is also that
which is humanly unknowable. In our relation to these two worlds there is plenty of
scope for unhappiness. But Faraday was
also emotionally happy. His marriage was
an unqualified success; he had good friends;
the tenor of his life was even and he did
not desire more than what he possessed. He
was equally fortunate in his relation to the
unknowable. The problems of life, as they
are called, never troubled him. The religion

in which he was brought up offered a solution of them in advance; he passed through no crisis such as that which drove Tolstoy almost to suicide. It is interesting to note that he separated the domain of science sharply from that of religion, the knowable from the unknowable. "Not *how* the world is, is the mystical, but *that* it is," says Wittgenstein. And again: "For an answer which cannot be expressed the question too cannot be expressed. The riddle does not exist. . . . The solution of the problem of life is seen in the vanishing of this problem. (Is not this the reason why men to whom after long doubting the sense of life became clear, could not then say wherein this sense consisted?)" Faraday was happy in that he never doubted, never tried to put an inexpressible question for which there is no possible answer. How the world is, he set himself to discover, with more success than attends most investigators. He did not torture his intellect with the question why or what it is. His religion offered him the explanation why; or to be more exact (for there is no explanation) it helped him to "contemplate the world *sub specie æterni*, as a limited whole." "The feeling of the world as a limited whole is the mystical feeling." Faraday had that feeling; not perhaps in its most exquisite form, but had it genuinely. His relations with the unknowable therefore were as satisfactory as his relations with what can be known.

Among the natural philosophers Faraday is by no means unique in his happiness. Indeed, as a class, I should say that men of science were happier than other men. *A priori*, and almost by definition, they ought to be. And when one reads their lives one finds that in point of fact they generally were happy. How satisfactory these lives of born men of science always are! There is an integrity about these men, a unity of purpose that to the rest of us poor distracted mortals seems wonderfully enviable and wonderfully beautiful.

If I could be born again and choose what I should be in my next existence, I should desire to be a man of science—not accidentally but by nature, inevitably a man of science. Fate might offer other alternatives—to have power or wealth, be a king or a statesman. These glittering temptations I should have small difficulty in rejecting; for my objection to the irritating turmoil of practical life is even stronger than my love of money or power, and since these cannot be obtained without plunging into practical life, I can sacrifice them cheerfully.

It is easy to make a virtue of psychological necessity. The only thing that might make me hesitate would be an offer by fate of artistic genius. But even if I could be Shakespeare, I think I should still choose to be Faraday. True, the posthumous glory of Shakespeare is greater than that of Faraday; men still read *Macbeth* but not (even if they happen to be electricians) the *Experimental Researches in Electricity*. The work of a man of science is a creation on which others build; it has implications, it grows. If we want to know about electricity, we read what the contemporary successors and disciples of Faraday have to say about it. But *Macbeth* is a thing in itself, not a discovery on which other men can improve. There is no such thing as progress in art. Every artist begins at the beginning. The man of science, on the other hand, begins where his predecessor left off. Opinions and ideas change, under the weight of accumulated experience, from age to age. The instinctive, emotional side of man, being hereditary, remains the same. The man of science provides the experience that changes the ideas of the race; in course of time his discoveries are superseded. The artist does not go out of date because he works with materials that do not change. Lyrics composed by a palæolithic poet would still be moving. But the views of a palæolithic astronomer would possess, for us, a merely historical and academic interest.

And yet in spite of all this I would still rather be Faraday than Shakespeare. Posthumous fame brings nobody much satisfaction this side of the grave; and though the consciousness that one possesses a great artistic talent must be profoundly satisfying, though the free employment of it must be a source of happiness, it seems to me that the possession and employment of a scientific talent must be still more satisfying. For the artist, whose function is the apt expression and the conveyance to others of the common human emotions, must fatally pass much of his life in the emotional world of human contacts. His reflections upon the world, his personal reactions to contacts—these form the subject matter of his art. The world in which the man of science passes the professional part of his life is non-human, has nothing to do with personal relationships and emotional reactions. We are all subdued to what we work in; and I personally would rather be subdued to intellectual contemplation than to emotion, would rather use my soul professionally for knowing than for feeling.

One of the minor disadvantages of being a great artist is the fact that the artist enjoys a considerable social prestige. Art is the subject of snobbery to a far greater extent than science. The presence of a well-known poet or painter is felt to give distinction to a dinner-party. Hostesses rarely ask one to meet bio-chemists, however distinguished. The reason for this is simple; all men and women imagine that they can appreciate the arts—and up to a point, of course, actually can—while the number who can understand the technicalities of science is remarkably small. (Vainly, alas, I wish that I myself belonged to that minority.) To this is due the enviable immunity of the men of science from the intrusion of frivolous bores. The artist, on the other hand, is one of the favourite quarries of the unemployed rich; a good specimen is worth at least an ambassador, almost an Indian prince. If the artist is a man of strong character he will find the attentions of the lion-hunters not dangerous, indeed, but profoundly exasperating. They are only dangerous to those who allow themselves to be caught. It is pleasant to be flattered; and if one likes to waste time, there is no easier way of doing so than in casual social intercourse. The artist who succumbs to social temptations loses everything: his time, his integrity, his sense of proportion, the very hope of achieving anything important. He is the more unfortunate in being exposed to them.

Towards morning when, like a mutton chop on a cold plate, I had a little thawed my bed, the phantoms of Michael Faraday and Sir Humphry Davy departed, leaving me alone with my repressed wishes. What they may have been, I don't know. But at any rate they fulfilled themselves, ideally and symbolically, in a confused nightmare of motor cars and snowdrifts.

The wind was still blowing when I woke up. We spent the forenoon shivering in the sitting-room of the inn. Every few minutes the landlord came in with fresh news about the state of affairs on the pass. Telephone messages had arrived from Florence and Bologna; an army of shovellers was being mobilized; now it was on the move; a man who had just come down from the pass had seen them at work; by two o'clock the road could not fail to be clear. After giving us each item of news, he bowed, smiled, rubbed his hands and went back to his kitchen to invent the next. He had a fertile imagination.

Fitfully, I read about the Armenian Church. But my interest was languid. I was too cold even to feel a proper enthusiasm over the discovery that "the old sacrificial hymns were probably obscene and certainly nonsensical." Remembering that phrase in subsequent summers, I have been delighted by it. How well, how pithily it describes not merely the old sacrificial hymns of pre-Christian Armenia, but a whole mass of modern art and self-styled science—the greater part of psycho-analytic literature, for example, the music of Schreker, most expressionist painting, *Ulysses*, and so on. As for the less "modern" pseudo-sciences and pseudo-art, from spiritualism to commercial fiction—these do not even possess the saving grace of obscenity; they are merely nonsensical.

The morning passed; it was time for lunch. After a meal of spaghetti and broiled goat, we felt a little stronger and a little less cold. "How are things on the pass?" we asked. But our host seemed suddenly to have lost his omniscience and with it his optimism. He did not know what was happening and he advised us to wait for a little. By five o'clock, however, all would undoubtedly be well. And the road by Firenzuola? That was hopeless; he was certain of that. He left us wondering what to do; whether to wait, whether to return

to Florence—what? We were still in a
state of painful uncertainty when a heaven-
sent messenger in the form of a man with
a horse and trap stopped at the inn door.
We appealed to him. A miracle! Not only
did he know the truth; he also imparted his
knowledge in a plain unvarnished way. No
shovellers, he assured us, were working on
the pass; nor would any be sent there till
the wind had changed (for when the wind
was blowing in this particular direction, the
snow was carried back on to the road as soon
as it had been taken off). The wind might
change this evening, of course; but on the
other hand it might only change next week.
But if we wanted to go to Bologna, why
hadn't we taken the Firenzuola road? Yes,
why not? said the landlord, who had joined
us and was listening to the conversation.
Why not take the Firenzuola road? He had
seen that the game was up and that there
was now no further hope of getting us to
stay another night. Why not? We looked
at him significantly, in silence. He smiled
back, imperviously good-humoured, and retired to compile his bill.

We set out. The sky was white and full
of cloudy movement. Here and there the
white mountains were scarred with black,
where the precipices were too steep to allow

the snow to lie. From La Casetta we slid down the break-neck road that twists down into the valley of the Santerno. Within its walls Firenzuola was black, ancient and grim. From Firenzuola the road follows the Santerno. The river has tunnelled a winding passage through the mountains. The valley is deep and narrow; here and there road and river run between perpendicular walls of rock, banded slantwise with the lines of tilted stratification. Slowly the valley broadens out, the mountains degenerate into bare bleak downs. At the foot of the hills is the plain, narrowed here between the mountains and the sea, but expanding and expanding as one travels northwards into the immense unbroken flatness of the Po valley.

At Imola we turned into the great Via Emilia that runs in an undeviating straight line from Rimini to Piacenza. What cities are strung along that white stretched thread! Cesena, Forli, Faenza, Imola, Bologna, Reggio, Modena, Parma—bead after precious bead.

It was dark when we entered Bologna and the streets were full of maskers. It was the last day of carnival.

We nosed our way through the crowd, hooting. "Maschere!" the maskers shouted

as we passed; and in our goggles and muf-
flers, we too seemed dressed for carnival.
It was a feeble show; a few young women in
dominoes, a few noisy students in fancy
dress—that was all. I thought of the brilliant shows and masquerades of the past.
Charming, no doubt; but one should not
regret them. For shows and masquerades
are symptoms of bad government. Tyrants
pass all their lives at the centre of a gorgeous
ballet. An oppressed populace, too poor to
pay for amusements of its own, is kept in
good humour by these royal theatricals,
which are free of charge. And in the course
of periodical Saturnalia slaves are able to
sublimate their revolutionary feelings in
sportive licence. If carnival has decayed, so
too has oppression. And where people have
pence enough to go to the cinema, there is
no need for kings and popes to stage their
ballets. Still, it was a very poor show; I
felt they might have celebrated our arrival
in Bologna a little more worthily.

WORK AND LEISURE

REFORMERS look forward to a time when efficient social organization and perfected machinery will do away with the necessity for severe and prolonged labour, making possible for all men and women an amount of leisure such as is enjoyed at the present day only by a privileged few. Nobody, in that golden age, will need to work more than four or five hours a day. The rest of every man's time will be his own, to do with whatsoever he likes.

It is difficult for any sensitive person not to sympathize with these aspirations. One must be most arrogantly certain of one's own super-manhood before one can complacently accept the slavery on which the possibility of being a super-man is based. Poor Nietzsche ended by signing his letters "Nietzsche Cæsar" and died in a madhouse. Perhaps that is the price that must be paid—at any rate by the intelligent; for the placidly stupid never pay, just as they never receive, anything—for an unfaltering conviction of superiority.

But sympathy with an ideal need not make the sympathizer uncritical of it; one may feel strongly, but one must not therefore cease to think. The majority of human beings are oppressed by excessive labour of the most senseless kind. That fact may, and indeed should, arouse our indignation and our pity. But these emotions must not prevent us from criticizing the project of those who wish to change the present state of things. The social reformers desire to see a dispensation under which all men will have as much, or nearly as much leisure as is enjoyed by the leisured classes to-day. We may be permitted to doubt, for all our sympathy, whether the consummation is really, after all, so much to be desired.

Let us begin by asking one simple question: What is it proposed that human beings shall do with the leisure which social reorganization and perfected machinery are to give them?

Prophets of the future give fundamentally the same answer to this question, with slight variations according to their different tastes. Henri Poincaré, for example, imagined that the human beings of the future would fill their long leisures by "contemplating the laws of nature." Mr. Bernard Shaw is of much the same opinion. Having ceased, by the time they are four years old, to take any interest in such childish things as love, art

and the society of their fellow beings, the
Ancients in *Back to Methuselah* devote their
indefinitely prolonged existences to meditat-
ing on the mysterious and miraculous beauty
of the cosmos. **Mr. H. G.** Wells portrays
in *Men like Gods* a race of athletic chemists
and mathematical physicists who go about
naked and, unlike Mr. Shaw's austerer
Ancients, make free love in a rational manner between the experiments. They also
take an interest in the arts and are not above
playing games.

These three answers to our question are
typical. Different prophets may differ in
their estimate of the relative importance of
the various activities which make up what is
generally known as "the higher life"; but all
agree that the lives of our leisured posterity
will be high. They will eagerly make themselves acquainted with "the best that has
been thought or said" about everything; they
will listen to concerts of the classiest music;
they will practise the arts and handicrafts
(at any rate until the time comes when even
these occupations seem childish); they will
study the sciences, philosophy, mathematics,
and meditate on the lovely mystery of the
world in which they live.

In a word, these leisured masses of a future which there is no reason to believe enor-

mously remote—indeed, our grandchildren may live to see the establishment of the four-hour day—will do all the things which our leisured classes of the present time so conspicuously fail to do.

How many rich and leisured people are there now living, who spend their time contemplating the laws of nature? I cannot say; all I know is that I rarely meet them. Many of the leisured, it is true, devote themselves to the patronage and even the amateur practice of the arts. But any one who has moved among rich "artistic" people knows how much of this cultivation of the arts is due to snobbery, how shallow and insincere their loudly voiced enthusiasms mostly are. The leisured classes take up art for the same reasons that they take up bridge—to escape from boredom. With sport and love-making, art helps to fill up the vacuum of their existence.

At Monte Carlo and Nice one meets the rich whose dominant interests are play and love. Two millions, according to my guide-book, annually visit Monte Carlo alone. Seven-eighths of the whole leisured population of Europe must concentrate themselves yearly on that strip of the coast. Five thousand jazz bands play daily for their delectation. A hundred thousand motor vehicles transport them from one place to another at great speed. Huge joint-stock companies offer them every kind of distraction, from roulette to golf. Legions of prostitutes assemble from all parts of the globe and enthusiastic amateurs of the gentle passion abound. For four months in the year the French Riviera is an earthly paradise. When the four months are over, the leisured rich return to their northerly homes, where they find awaiting them less splendid, but quite authentic *succursales* of the paradise they have left behind.

The leisured rich at Monte Carlo are those, I have said, whose chief resources against ennui or serious thoughts are love and play. Many of them are also "artistic." But it is not, I think, at Monte Carlo that the best specimens of the artistic rich are to be found. To see them at their best one must go to Florence. Florence is the home of those who cultivate with an equal ardour Mah Jong and a passion for Fra Angelico. Over tea and crumpets they talk, if they are too old for love themselves, of their lascivious juniors; but they also make sketches in water colour and read the *Little Flowers of St. Francis.*

I must not, in justice to the leisured rich, omit to mention that respectable minority of

them who occupy themselves with works of
charity (not to mention tyranny), with politics, with local administration and occasion-
ally with scholarly or scientific studies. I
hesitate to use the word "service"; for it has
been held up so frequently as an ideal and
by such a riff-raff of newspaper proprietors,
hard-headed business men and professional
moralists from the Y.M.C.A., that it has lost
all real significance. The "ideal of service"
is achieved, according to our modern mes-
siahs, by those who do efficient and profitable
business with just enough honesty to keep
them out of gaol. Plain shop-keeping is thus
exalted into a beautiful virtue. The ideal
of service which animates the best part of
the English leisured class has nothing to do
with the ideals of service so frequently mentioned by advertisers in American magazines.
If I had not made this clear, my praise might
have been thought, if not positively insult-
ing, at least most damnably faint.

There exists, then, an admirable minority.
But even when the minority and its occupations are duly taken into account, it cannot
honestly be said that the leisured classes of
the present time, or indeed of any historical
period of which we have knowledge, provide
a very good advertisement for leisure. The
contemplation of richly leisured life in

Monte Carlo and even in artistic Florence is by no means cheering or elevating.

Nor are we much reassured when we consider the occupations of the unleisured poor during those brief hours of repose allowed them between their work and their sleep. Watching other people play games, looking at cinema films, reading newspapers and indifferent fiction, listening to radio concerts and gramophone records and going from place to place in trains and omnibuses—these, I suppose, are the principal occupations of the working man's leisure. Their cheapness is all that distinguishes them from the diversions of the rich. Prolong the leisure, and what will happen? There will have to be more cinemas, more newspapers, more bad fiction, more radios and more cheap automobiles. If wealth and education increase with the leisure, then there will have to be more Russian Ballets as well as more movies, more *Timeses* as well as more *Daily Mails*, more casinos as well as more bookies and football matches, more expensive operas as well as more gramophone records, more Hugh Walpoles as well as more Nat Goulds. Acting on the same organisms the same causes may be expected to produce the same effects. And for all ordinary purposes, and so far as historical time is concerned, human nature is practically unchanging; the organism does remain the same. *Argal*, as Lancelot Gobbo would have said. . . .

This being so, we must further assume that increase of leisure will be accompanied by a correspondingly increased incidence of those spiritual maladies—ennui, restlessness, spleen and general world-weariness—which afflict and have always afflicted the leisured classes now and in the past.

Another result of increased leisure, provided that it is accompanied by a tolerably high standard of living, will be a very much increased interest on the part of what is now the working class in all matters of an amorous nature. Love, in all its complicated luxuriance, can only flourish in a society composed of well-fed, unemployed people. Examine the literature which has been written by and for members of the leisured classes and compare it with popular working class literature. Compare *La Princesse de Clèves* with *The Pilgrim's Progress*, Proust with Charles Garvice, Chaucer's *Troilus and Cressida* with the ballads. It becomes at once sufficiently evident that the leisured classes do take and have always taken a much keener and, I might say, more professional interest in love than the workers. A man cannot work hard and at the same time

conduct elaborate love affairs. Making love,
at any rate in the style in which unemployed
women desire it to be made, is a whole-time
job. It demands both energy and leisure.
Now energy and leisure are precisely the
things which a hard worker lacks. Reduce
his working hours and he will have both.

If, to-morrow or a couple of generations
hence, it were made possible for all human
beings to lead the life of leisure which is
now led only by a few, the results, so far
as I can see, would be as follows: There
would be an enormous increase in the demand for such time-killers and substitutes
for thought as newspapers, films, fiction,
cheap means of communication and wire-
less telephones; to put it in more general
terms, there would be an increase in the demand for sport and art. The interest in
the fine art of love-making would be widely
extended. And enormous numbers of people, hitherto immune from these mental and
moral diseases, would be afflicted by ennui,
depression and universal dissatisfaction.

The fact is that, brought up as they are
at present, the majority of human beings
can hardly fail to devote their leisure to
occupations which, if not positively vicious,
are at least stupid, futile and, what is worse,
secretly realized to be futile.

To Tolstoy the whole idea of universal leisure seemed absurd and even wicked. The social reformers who held up the attainment of universal leisure as an ideal he regarded as madmen. They aspired to make all men like those rich, idle, urban people among whom he had passed his youth and whom he so profoundly despised. He regarded them as conspirators against the welfare of the race.

What seemed to Tolstoy important was not that the workers should get more leisure but that the leisured should work. For him the social ideal was labour for all in natural surroundings. He wanted to see all men and women living on the land and subsisting on the produce of the fields that they themselves had tilled. The makers of Utopias are fond of prophesying that a time will come when men will altogether abandon agriculture and live on synthetic foods; to Tolstoy the idea was utterly revolting. But though he was doubtless right to be revolted, the prophets of synthetic food are probably better seers than he. Mankind is more likely to become urbanized than completely rural-ized. But these probabilities do not concern us here. What concerns us is Tolstoy's opinion of leisure.

Tolstoy's dislike of leisure was due to his

own experience as an idle youth and his observation of other rich and leisured men and women. He concluded that, as things are, leisure is generally more of a curse than a blessing. It is difficult, when one visits Monte Carlo or the other earthly paradises of the leisured not to agree with him. Most minds will only do work under compulsion. Leisure is only profitable to those who desire, even without compulsion, to do mental work. In a society entirely composed of such active minds leisure would be an unmixed blessing. Such a society has never existed and does not at the present exist. Can it ever be called into being?

Those who believe that all the defects of nature may be remedied by suitable nurture will reply in the affirmative. And indeed it is sufficiently obvious that the science of education is still in a very rudimentary condition. We possess a sufficient knowledge of physiology to be able to devise gymnastic exercises that shall develop the body to its highest attainable efficiency. But our knowledge of the mind, and particularly of the growing mind, is far less complete; and even such knowledge as we possess is not systematically or universally applied to the problems of education. Our minds are like the flabby bodies of sedentary city dwellers

—inefficient and imperfectly developed. With a vast number of people intellectual development ceases almost in childhood; they go through life with the intellectual capacities of boys or girls of fifteen. A proper course of mental gymnastics, based on real psychological knowledge, would at least permit all minds to reach their maximum development. Splendid prospect! But our enthusiasm for education is a little cooled when we consider what *is* the maximum development attainable by the greatest number of human beings. Men born with talents are to men born without them as human beings to dogs in respect to these particular faculties. Mathematically, I am a dog compared with Newton; a dog, musically, compared with Beethoven, and a dog artistically compared with Giotto. Not to mention the fact that I am a dog compared to Blondin, as a tight-rope walker; a billiard-playing dog compared with Newman; a boxing dog compared with Dempsey; a wine-tasting dog compared with Ruskin's father. And so on. Even if I were perfectly educated in mathematics, music, painting, tight-rope walking, billiard playing, boxing and wine-tasting, I should only become a trained dog instead of a dog in the state of nature. The prospect fills me with only moderate satisfaction.

Education can assure to every man the maximum of mental development. But is that maximum high enough in the majority of cases to allow a whole society to live in leisure without developing those deplorable qualities which have always characterized the leisured classes? I know plenty of people who have received the best education available in the present age and employ their leisure as though they had never been educated at all. But then our best education is admittedly bad (though good enough for all the men of talent and genius whom we possess); perhaps when it has been made really efficient, these people will spend their leisure contemplating the laws of nature. Perhaps. I venture to doubt it.

Mr. Wells, who is a believer in nurture, puts his Utopia three thousand years into the future; Mr. Shaw, less optimistically trusting to nature and a process of conscious evolution, removes his to the year 30,000 A.D. Geologically speaking, these times are to all intent equal in their brevity. Unfortunately, however, we are not fossils, but men. Even three thousand years seem, in our eyes, an uncommonly long time. The thought that, three thousand or thirty thousand years hence, human beings may, conceivably, be leading a lovely and rational existence is only mildly comforting and feebly sustaining. Men have a habit of thinking only of themselves, their children and their children's children. And they are quite right. Thirty thousand years hence, all may be well. But meanwhile that bad geological quarter of an hour which separates the present from that rosy future has got to be lived through. And I foresee that one of the minor, or even the major problems of that quarter of an hour will be the problem of leisure. By the year two thousand the six-hour day will be everywhere the rule, and the next hundred years will probably see the maximum reduced to five or even less. Nature, by then, will have had no time to change the mental habits of the race; and nurture, though improved, will only turn dogs into trained dogs. How will men and women fill their ever-expanding leisure? By contemplating the laws of nature, like Henri Poincaré? Or by reading the *News of the World?* I wonder.

POPULAR MUSIC

THERE is a certain jovial, bouncing, hoppety little tune with which any one who has spent even a few weeks in Germany, or has been tended in childhood by a German nurse, must be very familiar. Its name is "Ach, du lieber Augustin." It is a merry little affair in three-four time; in rhythm and melody so simple, that the village idiot could sing it after a first hearing; in sentiment so innocent that the heart of the most susceptible maiden would not quicken by a beat a minute at the sound of it. Rum ti-tiddle, Um tum tum, Um tum tum, Um tum tum: Rum ti-tiddle, Um tum tum, Um tum tum, TUM. By the very frankness of its cheerful imbecility the thing disarms all criticism.

Now for a piece of history. "Ach, du lieber Augustin" was composed in 1770, and it was the first waltz. The first waltz! I must ask the reader to hum the tune to himself, then to think of any modern waltz with which he may be familiar. He will find in the difference between the tunes a subject richly suggestive of interesting meditations.

The difference between "Ach, du lieber Augustin" and any waltz tune composed at any date from the middle of the nineteenth century onwards, is the difference between one piece of music almost completely empty of emotional content and another, densely saturated with amorous sentiment, languor and voluptuousness. The susceptible maiden who, when she hears "Ach, du lieber Augustin," feels no emotions beyond a general sense of high spirits and cheerfulness, is fairly made to palpitate by the luscious strains of the modern waltz. Her soul is carried swooning along, over waves of syrup; she seems to breathe an atmosphere heavy with ambergris and musk. From the jolly little thing it was at its birth, the waltz has grown into the voluptuous, heart-stirring affair with which we are now familiar.

And what has happened to the waltz has happened to all popular music. It was once innocent but is now provocative; once pellucid, now richly clotted; once elegant, now deliberately barbarous. Compare the music of *The Beggar's Opera* with the music of a contemporary revue. They differ as life in the garden of Eden differed from life in the artistic quarter of Gomorrah. The one is pre-lapsarian in its airy sweetness; the other is rich, luscious and loud with conscious savagery.

The evolution of popular music has run parallel on a lower plane, with the evolution of serious music. The writers of popular tunes are not musicians enough to be able to invent new forms of expression. All they do is to adapt the discoveries of original geniuses to the vulgar taste. Ultimately and indirectly, Beethoven is responsible for all the languishing waltz tunes, all the savage jazzings, for all that is maudlin and violent in our popular music. He is responsible because it was he who first devised really effective musical methods for the direct expression of emotion. Beethoven's emotions happened to be noble; moreover, he was too intellectual a musician to neglect the formal, architectural side of music. But unhappily he made it possible for composers of inferior mind and character to express in music their less exalted passions and vulgarer emotions. He made possible the weakest sentimentalities of Schumann, the baroque grandiosities of Wagner, the hysterics of Scriabine; he made possible the waltzes of all the Strausses, from the *Blue Danube* to the waltz from *Salome*. And he made possible, at a still further remove, such masterpieces of popu-

lar art as "You made me love you" and
"That old black mammy of mine."

For the introduction of a certain vibrant
sexual quality into music, Beethoven is perhaps less directly responsible than the nineteenth-century Italians. I used often to
wonder why it was that Mozart's operas
were less popular than those of Verdi,
Leoncavallo and Puccini. You couldn't ask
for more infectiously "catchy" tunes than
are to be found in *Figaro* or *Don Gio-
vanni*. The music though "classical," is not
obscure, nor forbiddingly complex. On the
contrary it is clear, simple with that seemingly easy simplicity which only consummate genius can achieve and thoroughly en-
gaging. And yet for every time *Don Gio-
vanni* is played, *La Bohème* is played a hundred. *Tosca* is at least fifty times as popular as *Figaro*. And if you look through a
catalogue of gramophone records you will
find that, while you can buy *Rigoletto* complete in thirty discs, there are not more than
three records of *The Magic Flute*. This
seems at first sight extremely puzzling. But
the reason is not really far to seek. Since
Mozart's day composers have learned the art
of making music throatily and palpitatingly
sexual. The arias of Mozart have a beautiful clear purity which renders them utterly

insipid compared with the sobbing, catch-in-the-throaty melodies of the nineteenth-century Italians. The public, having accustomed itself to this stronger and more turbid brewage, finds no flavour in the crystal songs of Mozart.

No essay on modern popular music would be complete without some grateful reference to Rossini, who was, so far as I know, the first composer to show what charms there are in vulgar melody. Melodies before Rossini's day were often exceedingly commonplace and cheap; but almost never do they possess that almost indefinable quality of low vulgarity which adorns some of the most successful of Rossini's airs, and which we recognize as being somehow a modern, contemporary quality. The methods which Rossini employed for the achievement of his melodic vulgarity are not easy to analyse. His great secret, I fancy, was the very short and easily memorable phrase frequently repeated in different parts of the scale. But it is easiest to define by example. Think of Moses' first Aria in *Moses in Egypt*. That is an essentially vulgar melody; and it is quite unlike the popular melodies of an earlier date. Its affinities are with the modern popular tune. It is to his invention of vulgar tunes that Rossini owed his enor-

mous contemporary success. Vulgar people
before his day had to be content with
Mozart's delicate airs. Rossini came and
revealed to them a more congenial music.
That the world fell down and gratefully
worshipped him is not surprising. If he has
long ceased to be popular, that is because his
successors, profiting by his lessons, have
achieved in his own vulgar line triumphs of
which he could not have dreamed.

Barbarism has entered popular music from
two sources—from the music of barbarous
people, like the negroes, and from serious
music which has drawn upon barbarism for
its inspiration. The technique of being barbarous effectively has come, of course, from
serious music. In the elaboration of this
technique no musicians have done more than
the Russians. If Rimsky Korsakoff had
never lived, modern dance music would not
be the thing it is.

Whether, having grown inured to such
violent and purely physiological stimuli as
the clashing and drumming, the rhythmic
throbbing and wailing glissandos of modern
jazz music can supply, the world will ever
revert to something less crudely direct, is a
matter about which one cannot prophesy.
Even serious musicians seem to find it hard
to dispense with barbarism. In spite of the

monotony and the appalling lack of subtlety which characterize the process, they persist in banging away in the old Russian manner, as though there were nothing more interesting or exciting to be thought of. When, as a boy, I first heard Russian music, I was carried off my feet by its wild melodies, its persistent, its relentlessly throbbing rhythms. But my excitement grew less and less with every hearing. To-day no music seems to me more tedious. The only music a civilized man can take unfailing pleasure in is civilized music. If you were compelled to listen every day of your life to a single piece of music, would you choose Stravinsky's "Oiseau de Feu" or Beethoven's "Grosse Fugue"? Obviously, you would choose the fugue, if only for its intricacy and because there is more in it to occupy the mind than in the Russian's too simple rhythms. Composers seem to forget that we are, in spite of everything and though appearances may be against us, tolerably civilized. They overwhelm us not merely with Russian and negroid noises, but with Celtic caterwaulings on the black notes, with dismal Spanish wailings, punctuated by the rattle of the castanets and the clashing harmonies of the guitar. When serious composers have gone back to civilized music—and already some of them are turning from barbarism—we shall probably hear a corresponding change for the more refined in popular music. But until serious musicians lead the way, it will be absurd to expect the vulgarizers to change their style.

ONCE, in the course of an ill-spent life, it was my fate to go to the theatre some two hundred and fifty times in one year. On business, I need not add; one would hardly do that sort of thing for pleasure. I was paid to go.

By the end of the year—and, for that matter, long before our planet had completed its orbit round the sun—I had come to the conclusion that I was not paid enough; that, indeed, I could never be paid enough for this particular job. I gave it up; and nothing would now induce me to resume it.

Since then, my attendances at the theatre have averaged perhaps three per annum.

And yet there are people who go to every first night, not because they have to, not because the griping belly must be filled, but because they like it. They are not paid to go; they pay, as though for a privilege. The ways of men are indeed strange.

Concerning this mystery, I used often to speculate—abstracting myself as completely as I could from the environing horrors—during the most excruciating passages of the plays which I had to attend. Sitting all

round me in the stalls—it was thus I used
to reflect—are several hundred prosperous
and, as education goes, well-educated people,
who have paid money to see this drivelling
play; (for I am assuming that the play is
one of the nineteen drivelling ones and not
the rare twentieth *Heartbreak House* or *At
Mrs. Beam's*). They are the sort of people
who, in the privacy of their homes, would
read the better class of novels, or at any
rate not the worst. They would be indig-
nant if you offered them a penny novelette.

And yet these readers of respectable fiction
will go to the theatre (under no compulsion,
be it remembered) to see plays which, as
literature, are precisely on a level with the
penny novelettes they scorn, very rightly and
naturally, to read.

In their novels they demand a certain
minimum of probability, truth to life, credi-
ble characterization and decent writing. An
impossible story, in which the personages are
so many dolls, moving in obedience to the
laws of an absurd and outworn convention
and expressing themselves in a grotesque,
tumid and ungrammatical English—this
would disgust them. But to a play answer-
ing precisely to this description, they will
flock in their thousands. They will be
moved to tears and enthusiasm by situations

which, in a novel, they would find merely
ludicrous.   They will let pass, and even
fervidly admire, language which any one
with the slightest feeling for the use of
words would shudder to see in print.

It was over this strange anomaly that I
used to ponder during those hideous evenings
at the theatre.   Why does the penny novelette disgust, in book form, those who delight
in it when exhibited on the stage?   Put
succinctly, that was the not uninteresting
problem.

Mr. Bernard Shaw has said that it is
easier to write a novel than a play; and to
show with what horrible facility a novelist
can spin out into pages of thin description
what the dramatist must compress into a few
lines of dialogue, he re-wrote in modern nar-
rative form a scene from *Macbeth*.   Admittedly, Shakespeare stood the comparison
very well.   For it is certainly easier to write
a bad novel than a good play.   But on the
other hand, it is much easier to write a bad
play that will be successful—even with a
quite intelligent and discriminating audience
—than a bad novel that will take in readers
of the same class.   A dramatist can "get
away with" a play in which there is no
characterization subtler than caricature, no
beauty of language less coarse than ranting

rhetoric, no resemblance to life—only an effective situation. The novelist cannot.

This fact was recently impressed upon me (yet once more) when I went to the theatre in Parma—not, alas, the great Estensian theatre, but a gimcrack little modern playhouse—to see the Italian version of one of Sir Arthur Pinero's plays—*His House in Order* it is called, if I remember rightly, in English. I confess that I thoroughly enjoyed the performance. English *Higlif*, as seen through the eyes of an Italian touring company was worth coming far—all the way from England—to study. And the comedians were admirable. But I marvelled, as I listened, that a piece so entirely empty—for at Parma the unconscious humour and the good acting were merely accidental additions to the blank original—could have been, could still be, such a success. And as a hard-working novelist, I envied the lucky playwrights who can turn out a popular and even highly esteemed piece, in which the personages are either wooden puppets or caricatures, the language rant, and the plot a succession of those cheap epigrams of circumstance known as "situations." If I were allowed to make a novel out of only these ingredients, I should congratulate myself on having got off uncommonly cheaply.

What makes it possible for the dramatist to put so little into his plays, and yet successfully "get away with it," is, of course, the intervention of living interpreters. If he knows the trick—and one learns by practice—the dramatist can pass on to the actor the greater part of his responsibilities. All that he need do, if he is lazy, is to invent effective situations and leave the actors to make the most of them. Characterization, truth to life, ideas, decent writing and all the rest, he can resign to the writers for print, secure in the knowledge that the public will be too much taken up with the antics of the players to remark the absence of these merely literary trifles.

For it is the players, of course, who reconcile an otherwise relatively discriminating public to the sad stuff which finds its way on to the stage. It is for the sake of the comedians that occupants of the stalls who might, if they were sitting by their own firesides, be reading, shall we say, Wells or Conrad, or D. H. Lawrence, or even Dostoievsky are content to put up with the dramatic equivalent of the penny novelette and the picture-paper serial story; for the sake of the living, smiling comedians; for the personal touch, the palpitating human note.

If acting were always first class, I could

understand people becoming hardened first-nighters—or shouldn't one rather say "softened"? for the contemporary theatre is more relaxing than tonic, more emollient than astringent—becoming, then, softened first-nighters. A fine piece of acting is as well worth looking at as a fine performance in any other branch of art.

But good actors are as rare as good painters or good writers. Not more than two or three of the very best appear in every generation. I have seen a few. Old Guitry, for example. And Marie Lloyd, the marvellous, rich, Shakespearean Marie, now dead—alas, too soon; *car elle était du monde où les plus belles choses ont le pire destin.* And Little Tich. And Raquel Meller, marvellous both as diseuse and cinema actress, the most refined, the most nobly aristocratic interpreter of passion I have ever seen; *une âme bien née* if ever there was one. And Charlie Chaplin. All men and women of genius.

Such perfect performances as theirs are of course worth watching. And there are plenty of smaller talents, not to be despised. I am as willing to pay money to see these comedians interpreting nonsense as to pay to see a good play badly acted (and it is extraordinary how actor-proof a really good play can be). But why any one should pay to see a poor, or even very competent but un-inspired piece of acting in conjunction with a bad play—that is completely beyond my powers to understand.

Hardened—I beg your pardon—softened first-nighters to whom I have put this riddle have never been able to give me very satis-factory answers. Your true first-nighter, I can only presume, is born with a passion for the theatre; he loves it always, for its own sake, blindly (for love is blind), uncriti-cally. He pays his money at the box office, he. leaves his judgment in the cloak-room along with his great-coat, hat and walking stick, and takes his seat, certain that he will enjoy himself, whatever may happen on the stage. The stuffiness and the crowd, the dark, expectant hush and then the apoca-lyptic rising of the curtain, the glitter and the shining, painted unreality—these are enough in themselves to make him happy. He does not ask for more. I envy him his easily contented mind.

THE END